Michael Gannon is a retired trade journalist, living in Fulham. Born in Hammersmith, he has had a number of plays performed at his local fringe theatre. Gannon is currently writing a sequel to *Travails with Thomas: To Russia with Love*. This is concerning a trip with Thomas to the Balkans in 1989, immediately prior to the collapse of the communist regimes there.

Among his interests are theatre, classical music, current affairs and an undying support of Fulham FC.

To Little Dave, sadly missed.

Michael Gannon

TRAVAILS WITH THOMAS: TO RUSSIA WITH LOVE

AUSTIN MACAULEY PUBLISHERS™

LONDON ∗ CAMBRIDGE ∗ NEW YORK ∗ SHARJAH

A CIP catalogue record for this title is available from the British Library.

ISBN 9781398429260 (Paperback)
ISBN 9781398429277 (ePub e-book)

www.austinmacauley.com

First Published 2022
Austin Macauley Publishers Ltd®
1 Canada Square
Canary Wharf
London
E14 5AA

When I considered writing this work, I realised that trying to recreate a period and places that have changed so much – but in a humorous way – would need a great deal of research. This I have attempted to do but of particular note should be the friends who have voiced their opinions. Standing out in this is my great friend, Nancy Webber, who has helped enormously with her own expertise in book publishing.

Foreword

Travelling to what was the Eastern Bloc[1] had always been an attraction for me. While most of my friends preferred to flop down on a Greek island or a Costa, the thought of visiting countries that were regarded as threats to our way of life, let alone being Marxist-Leninist[2], proved too alluring to resist.

My luck was in, however, when I persuaded a friend in the Civil Service. He also wanted cities and culture to the sun-kissed beaches and agreed to come with me on what was deceptively termed 'A Grand Tour of Russia', organised at the time by Cosmos Tours. A 17-day coach trip would only have about eight days in the Soviet Union itself; the rest of the holiday would be going through Belgium, stopping off in Berlin and Warsaw on the way. But there were also to be stays in Minsk, Moscow, Novgorod and Leningrad before coming out into Finland.

There was an ulterior motive for me because I intended to try to see if I could meet the former in-laws of a disastrous marriage to a woman from Warsaw. But more of that in the novel.

The character of Thomas is based on a dear friend of mine who died some years ago, and I was always grateful that he was prepared to go on such trips. On the flip side, there was a need to keep an eye on him when alcoholic intake reached certain, critical levels. The pun of the title of the novel should indicate that.

Many of the incidents on this trip occurred as they are described, while others are creations of a fertile – or some would argue, febrile – mind. Our Belgian coach driver really was an amorous man who conquered as he went, while the guide was a diffident person whose leanings were in complete contrast to his colleague's. Both the Thomas character and myself had arguments on the trip, especially with 'Rick', a man who embodied all that was loathsome in American superiority long before the rise of Donald Trump.

What remains a source of constant wonder is that none of us on that trip could have imagined the disappearance of communism in Europe as quickly as it occurred. As I stood in 1984, casting my eyes over the depressing sight of the Berlin Wall[3], there was no hint that five years later it would come tumbling down. The control of the Communist Party in the Soviet Union appeared equally indestructible, even though it was afflicted by an ageing leadership and an economy that was straining to keep up in the arms race with the USA.

And the individual people we met during our fleeting visit often left us wondering. The Poles really did think Margaret Thatcher[4] and Ronald Reagan[5] were the best thing since sliced bread. When I mentioned we had unemployment of over three million, there would often be a shrug of their shoulders. Given the Eastern Bloc countries offered 'full' employment, anything less was seen as a problem solely for westerners. The Russians, including our Intourist[6] guide, Dina, were more guarded in their comments about how life was in the Soviet Union to the point of denying what we had discovered for ourselves, for instance being offered girls for sex in a Minsk hotel by two local wide guys.

For those of you who recall this period, I hope the novel will bring back memories. For those who were born after 1989, yes, there really was a time when an alternative to capitalism, albeit an imperfect one, tried but failed to deliver for those living beyond the Iron Curtain[7].

I have provided some of the important events that happened in 1984 immediately below. The endnotes at the back should be of use to those readers who may not be familiar with terms and historic persons who played their part in this extraordinary period.

I apologise for those who are well versed in their contemporary history, but it has been pointed out that many younger readers of this novel would not have a clue what and whom I am referring to. Although this might make the novel look like the reference books that often sent me to sleep during my studies at university, I hope, nevertheless, they prove useful. Ignore them if they don't.

Some Events of 1984

25 January – The UK government prohibits staff at GCHQ intelligence centre in Cheltenham from belonging to any trade union.

13 February – Konstantin Chernenko succeeds the late Yuri Andropov as General Secretary of the Communist Party of the Soviet Union.

12 March – Start of the miners' strike that sees Margaret Thatcher's government prepared to take on the National Union of Mineworkers (NUM) and its leader, Arthur Scargill, over the next year, to defeat the country's strongest union and fundamentally undermine organised labour's strength.

23 April – US researchers publish the discovery of the HIV/AIDS virus.

8 May – The Soviet Union declares it will boycott the 1984 Summer Olympics to be held in Los Angeles, USA, in July and August that year.

11 August – During a voice check for a radio broadcast, President Ronald Reagan jokingly states: "My fellow Americans, I'm pleased to tell you today that I've signed legislation that will outlaw Russia forever. We begin bombing in five minutes."

13 August – Home Secretary, Leon Brittan, accuses the NUM leadership of organising flying pickets as 'thugs', following his earlier denunciation of Arthur Scargill when he said there was no place for the 'dictatorial personal leadership' of the miners' leader.

10 October – Feature film of George Orwell's novel, *1984*, starring John Hurt, is released. Thatcher states the year 1984 in actuality is one of hope and possibility.

12 October – The Provisional IRA attempts to assassinate Margaret Thatcher and the Cabinet during the Conservative Party Conference in Brighton at the Grand Hotel. While she and her Cabinet survive, five people are killed with 31 injured.

Chapter One
London, March 1984

Thomas waited, fumbling nervously with his tie and looking at the wall in front of him where a portrait of the current Home Secretary was propped up against it and seemed to fix him with a sneering glare.

There was something off-putting about the man who had fawned his way into the favour of the PM and always gave the impression of someone who treated his subordinates with an air of condescension verging on contempt. Not that Tom had caught anything but fleeting sights of his ultimate boss, stomping down the corridor, correcting his aides as he went.

He coughed and cleared his throat and seeing a mirror on the wall, approached it and straightened his tie, pleased he had managed to get the Windsor knot correct this time. Tom patted his hair a little and considered what he saw. Yes, he fitted most people's view of a civil servant in his mid-thirties going nowhere fast. His thin nose just about supported the heavy glasses and he had noticed in recent years either his forehead was getting bigger, or his forelocks thinner. His stature was small, but no one could accuse him of being a midget. Yet, he detested being called at late night office parties as 'Tom Thumb'. It had started off as a joke, but he had made the big mistake of telling his friends outside his job and so the nickname stuck.

He took another look in the mirror and sighed. His skin was drawn tight and seemed to make his every look and expression impassive, even when he thought he was making his feelings clear. No, there was no getting away from it; even if he had dressed in the most colourful clown's outfit and makeup, he would still be regarded as anonymous.

"Tom, we're ready for you."

He hadn't noticed his boss opening the office door and the words made him jump back from the mirror. He nodded and entered the room gingerly while his superior shut the door behind him and invited him to sit down. Another man was at his desk, scrutinising a form and barely looked up as Tom mumbled a greeting.

"Ah, yes, thanks for coming for this little talk, Thomas," the seated man said, holding up the form, "and for your application here for your trip. Mr Morrison and I have had a quick look and would like to have a chat with you about it."

"Yes, Tom, this is all very informal, you understand, and Mr Worsthorne and I want to make it clear that the choice is entirely yours," explained Morrison, who had taken up his accustomed position, standing by his boss.

"Oh, let's make it really informal then, shall we, Charles?" suggested Worsthorne, getting out of his chair and going to the drinks cabinet, looking back to ask what they wanted.

"Oh, thank you, perhaps a whisky," said Tom, grateful for the offer.

"Really? Whisky? Thought it might be vodka." Worsthorne's guffaw filled the office, quickly followed by Morrison's.

Worsthorne came back with the drinks, sat heavily back down on his fine leather chair and looked at Tom. "Can I keep it informal and call you Tom, while you can still call me 'Mr Worsthorne' instead of 'sir'?"

"Thank you, sir," said a more relaxed Tom, raising his glass to his superior.

Worsthorne put his hands behind his head, swung his chair to face the big window and watched the pigeons winging their way down a grey, drizzly Whitehall.

"Gather you were in Northern Ireland before here and did some useful work during the hunger strikes. Difficult times. I suppose it must seem a bit tame here compared with bandit country and men in berets and dark glasses."

"Well, it—"

"But that's not what we're here to discuss," continued Worsthorne, not waiting for an answer. "No, we're here to discuss holidays!" he declared, swinging back to face Tom. "No berets, unless in Paris and sunglasses, not dark glasses, eh? Where are you off to come summer, Charles?"

"We're yodelling off to the Tyrol, Frank."

"I'm sure the hills will be alive with the sound of music when you do. I'm heading off solo down to Cape Town. Much against the Good Lady's wishes with those bombs going off and the ANC stirring things up again, but we have enough of that with the savages elsewhere, don't we, Tom?"

"Seeing the usual sights, Frank?"

"Oh, I'll be left off the hook with the missus back here, Charles, after visiting favoured son, might make a few sorties to Sun City," said a smiling Worsthorne to his colleague, twiddling his thumbs and then placing an index finger by his nose with a knowing wink. "Mind you, chances are I might have to put off Bongo Bongo Land if this strike gets really dirty with the miners. Which I think it might from what Leon keeps warning us about. See the kerfuffle with the Kent lot turned back at the Dartford Tunnel last week?"

"Frank, I really think we needn't bother Tom with our headaches over Scargill & Co."

Worsthorne nodded and clasped his hands, this time in front of him and looked Tom up and down.

"So, we're to have our own 007 jetting off to Bolshieland!"

"It's, it's a 17-day coach trip to the Soviet Union in August, and yes, fully escorted."

"Yes, it's the escorting side we wondered about. Now, you may be a small cog in our departmental wheel, Tom, but have you thought of what might lie in store for you once you get past the Iron Curtain, eh?"

Tom was increasingly aware that despite his strongest attempt at self-control, beads of sweat were appearing on his brow, and he reached inside his pocket for a handkerchief and dabbed away.

"We get picked up at Victoria and then our first stop is in Berlin." Tom realised his mouth was dry and while he talked, he swallowed and smacked his lips. "Er, West Berlin, that is. Then Warsaw and it's Minsk for the first night in the Soviet Union."

"And then, Tom?" queried Morrison.

"Oh, some time in Moscow, then Leningrad and we—"

"*We?*" queried Worsthorne.

"That's me and my friend, John."

"He's in the Civil Service too?" asked Morrison.

"Um, no, we met at university. Er, he's a…well…a journalist."

Tom watched as his superiors exchanged glances and raised their eyebrows.

"He works in the trade press…building press to be precise," said Tom hurriedly. "So, it's all right; he's not a *real* journalist."

Noting their expressions of relief, Tom felt reassured enough to continue with the itinerary. "And then we go on to Finland, Denmark and so on. We're only in the Soviet Union itself for about eight days—"

"*And* nights, my boy!" observed Worsthorne. "You're bound to go out and try the hotel bars, night clubs and whatever, aren't you, surely? Know I would at your age."

"Well, I suppose so."

"You see, Tom, we wonder if you might fall prey to a Russian blonde in some kind of honey trap sting," warned Morrison.

"Do you really think so?" asked Tom, leaning forward with unintended eagerness and louder smacking lips.

"You're a prime target," confirmed Worsthorne, although when he looked at Tom again, he squinted and cleared his throat. "We've had quite a few of our boys thinking they were helping detente with a Svetlana and blow me – so to speak – the prints arrive in the post showing all sorts of gymnastics snapped by the KGB's[8] David Bailey[9]. I hate to think of the look on your face if Postman Pat arrives with something similar addressed to Comrade Thomas Laurel, what?"

Tom was in deep thought at the graphically drawn prospect when he heard Worsthorne continue. "I can tell by the look on your face you'd be petrified."

"What Mr Worsthorne is saying," began Morrison as he walked past Tom to open the door, "is that we hope you enjoy the holiday but be aware that all may not be as it seems. And if things go pear-shaped, you can always try and contact us or…"

"Send us a postcard a day, eh?" joked Worsthorne, chuckling. "Wish you were here in the Lubyanka instead of me!"

"Perhaps we can have a chat with you when you get back," suggested Morrison, gently tapping Tom's shoulder as he reached and opened the door. "Oh and do remember to send my love to Olga on the Volga and especially Smasher Natasha."

"Charles, is he all right? He keeps on making that smacking sound."

The phone started ringing at 4.30 am, drowning out the dawn chorus and the man in the bed reluctantly answered it, lifting the receiver up and growling, "Who is it?"

"Sorry to trouble you at this time of evening, John, but I thought you'd be interested to know I got the all clear at the department today."

"It's bloody 4.30 in the morning, Thomas. It's Saturday *morning*, for God's sake! What are you playing at?"

There was silence down the other end and a clearing of the throat.

"Ah…morning, is it? I must have just woken up. Sorry."

"Just woken up?" John heard a noise at the other end of what sounded to be a glass smashing on the floor. "Have you been on the sauce?"

"Perhaps we can discuss this when you're less, er...um, agitated. Sorry, sorry," said Tom quickly, putting down the phone.

He focused his bleary eyes on the telephone and snorted. Had he really made such a mistake over the time of day? He tried rising from the chair, then collapsed back into it and surveyed the room. It was normally immaculate, but the cleaner hadn't been this week and there seemed to be several empty wine bottles strewn about.

He gazed down at the smashed glass and noticed the spilled contents that were staining the carpet. Mrs Pilkington had warned him about it before and said she shouldn't be expected to clean up after his binges. But didn't he have the right to celebrate this official approval of his trip?

He looked towards the fine old grandfather clock at the other side of the room and acknowledged that its hands showed John was right about the time, but surely, it was afternoon and not early morning? Tom managed to ease himself up from the armchair and hesitantly walk towards the big window, which in the daytime gave a beautiful view of the river and its weeping willows that his friends said they envied.

They brushed aside his belief that it was spoilt by the noisy wine bar below and the raucous noise that went on well after closing time, especially during the summer months. The yuppies bellowed and brayed at one another as the night wore on, whether they were female or male. The women had their puffed out shoulder pads and frizzy hair, *Dynasty* style, while the men circled around them like the alpha males he detested at work who always succeeded in getting their way.

This Victorian converted pump house looked idyllic at a casual glance but had disadvantages. Yes, it was situated in a beautiful part of West London and the journey to work in Whitehall was easy on the Underground but the hedonistic antics of these people below irritated him.

Yet none more than those from the flat next door. The couple seemed oblivious that the all too thin walls allowed him to listen at great length to their getting to know one another at any time of day or night. If they had even acknowledged his existence, it would have been something, but there was not a hint of a hello from either as they passed him, their heads buried in their Filofaxes.

His eyes widened in disbelief as at that precise moment he heard murmuring sounds mounting on the other side of the wall as he drew close to it. "Oh, God, Jez…Oh, God, Jez…!" Followed by: "Urrhh, Giselle! Urrhh, Giselle!" To his mounting disgust, the two merged into a discordant, carnal duet that made him decide it was time to open another bottle of wine and search for a glass. He kept his baleful eyes on the wall and listened to the sounds, which subsided and then resumed.

For the next half hour, Jez and Giselle managed to make not only their ardour known fully to Tom but tested the bedsprings to apparent destruction. All of a sudden, there was an almighty crash, and Tom could barely stifle a triumphant squeal of delight, almost jumping in the air and raising his glass high before taking a deep gulp of wine, licking his rouge-coloured lips. Should he call for an ambulance now or let the couple struggle to untie themselves from their grotesque coupling? His smirk at the thought lasted barely a moment because to his disbelief he heard through the wall: "Urrhh, Giselle! Urrhh, Giselle!" Followed by: "Jez…Oh, God…Oh, God, Jez…!"

He managed to get up from the chair and wave a fist at the wall and shout: "You bastards, it'll be the bloody floor that'll give way next!"
The harshness of his voice appeared to silence them momentarily. He set his chin, while his nostrils flared to show the authority that he believed he had conveyed, until his legs began to buckle. On the way to meeting the floor, he heard a coquettish female voice suggest: "I say, before it does, would you like to join us for a threesome?"

Chapter Two

"Can you all group around me, please? Yes, gather around me."

Tom and John obeyed the call and about 40 people circled around the man collecting the papers as the wind blew and it began to drizzle. "Now, 'ave you all got your papers with you? And I take it you 'ave all remembered your passports and you 'ave your visas?"

John looked at Tom quizzically.

"Yes, I have," came the terse reply.

"You were walking out without it when I called to check," noted John, looking down at his companion.

Not many people would have guessed the two were obvious friends. John was three or four inches taller and sported a dark beard and a developing beer gut, while Tom was wiry and fair in complexion. (Due to a car accident when he was young that had mangled his right leg, John had a noticeable limp.) Unless drink had been taken, it tended to be John who took the initiative while out and about and his friend followed along with whatever course of action he suggested.

So it had been with the idea of this holiday, which John had spotted on a visit to the travel agent. As he flicked through one particular brochure, his eyes had alighted on the trip to the Soviet Union and the opportunities to look at the familiar sites of Red Square and Peterhof in Leningrad. None of this would have appealed to his other friends, but Tom proved worth a try.

His mind drifted back to the time when he had gone behind the Iron Curtain for a visit to Poland four years before. His misfortune was that he ended up with first-hand experience of the Polish capacity at the time to see the West as a land of milk and honey.

A colleague at work had said he was still in contact with people he had met in the mid-1970s when money and life were relatively easy in that country and the two had set off to the land of lengthening food queues. The trip had been fascinating because they were staying with a professional Polish couple living on the outskirts of Warsaw who seemed to have all the western goods and where the word 'queue' was a foreign concept.

In 1980, Poland presented a strange image to a visitor from a country like the UK. Here was a communist country where anyone from the West was a fool not to use the black market when currency could be exchanged at seven or eight times the official rate. John overcame his initial qualms, and when his pounds became zlotys, he and his friend started living the lifestyle of millionaires, visiting the posh hotels and restaurants.

But as he looked around the bars in swanky places like the Warsaw Hilton, he noticed many pretty girls by themselves, drinking slowly and eyeing up the men coming through the doors.

On the second day in Warsaw, his friend, Tim, suggested going to a nightclub in the Hotel Bristol near the Old Town, where he had spent some evenings in the 1970s. What greeted him and John was a hotel that appeared closed but for the nightclub. What greeted them took their breath away. The music assaulted their ears, and they were in a room full of heavily painted women, who were regarding them in a way that John could not remember experiencing in London discos. Cigarette smoke wafted up and clung to the ceiling and the different perfumes and odours hit the two of them immediately, causing John, for one, to recoil.

"Are these women…are they…er, on the…?" he stuttered. "Warsaw seems to be crawling with them, Tim."

"Looks like it," confirmed his friend. "Changed a bit since I was last here."

John went to the bar to order, and as the barman answered in English to his '*Dwa piwa prosz*' (Two beers, please), he could detect the smell of heavy, cheap perfume, followed by a foot that touched his shin and rubbed against. There was an amused voice that whispered in his ear. "*Nie zapominaj, |e jestem zbyt spragniony.*" (Don't forget that I'm thirsty too.) He looked to his right and saw a woman smiling at him with her elbow on the bar and a hand under her chin. She had short, curly blonde hair and attractive blue eyes that did not seem too sly despite the suggestive moves of her foot against his leg.

"You're naughty," he said back to her in English as the beers arrived, and he indicated to the bartender that the lady's glass needed filling. At once, the other foot snaked around his leg, locking him in a tight grasp.

"You're *very* naughty," he insisted, but his words merely encouraged her to warmly embrace him in her arms.

"What is your name?" she asked in English, pecking him on the cheek. When he told her, she replied: "My name is Evonne."

She looked over her shoulder and saw John's friend dancing with a friend of hers, and as they swung by them, she continued: "And she is Evonne Two. Please, dance with me, *please*."

The music was slow, and it gave John time to assess his surroundings. The place was wall to wall with women and a few men being treated to close attention as they bargained on the rates. As John and Evonne Two danced by, he saw a girl give him an alluring smile, sticking her tongue out at him, wiggling it and indicating there was room to sit down by her. Lord, there was little doubting it; it was like no disco in London he had known. He looked back at Evonne whose arms were around his neck making it impossible for him to slip away.

"You come from where?" she asked.

"England…London."

"Nice, very nice. I welcome to see you in London?" His boggling eyes amused her. "Don't worry, I know…I am business girl and you respectable man. You have wife in London?"

"No."

"Girlfriend?"

"Afraid not."

"Oh, maybe Evonne One can be your wife here? As long as you not like Arab men. They not very nice to me. I don't like them. They are like animals to us."

Evonne stopped dancing and lifted a sleeve to show a dark, ugly bruise running down her arm. John looked at it and then by her right cheek saw it had been covered in more make up that almost hid another bruise.

"I'm so sorry," he started, briefly touching her face. "If I could—"

"Come back before our drinks are taken," she suggested, leading him by the hand to the bar. She raised the glass to him and continued, "No, you have need for a girl sophisticated, not me, John. I hope, I hope very much it…I mean, she come soon for you."

"Hello, you are English? Please let me practise mine."

John made room for the woman to sit down. It was the night after the Hotel Bristol visit and this time their Polish hosts had chosen a more respectable nightclub venue. This one appeared to have a normal clientele and feeling to it. The woman nodded and shook hands and took the seat John was indicating.

"Hello, my name is Ewelina. And you are?…John? John, I see, very good. And you are here in Poland for…?"

"Only a week. I am with my friend over there," he pointed quickly to where Tim was standing with their hosts, Pavel and Danuta. "I wanted to see what life was like in a communist country."

"Oh, it's bad here. What do you do?"

"I'm a journalist. And you?"

"Yes, me too."

That seemed like a fortunate coincidence, and John took a longer look at his newfound companion. She looked in her late twenties, had untamed, long brown hair and her makeup showed none of the gaudiness of the women in the Hotel Bristol. Her face was not in itself memorable; she had a thin nose and while the cheekbones were pronounced, her eyes were greyish and only came to life when she was amused. But John could not deny there was something about her that attracted him. She saw him looking at her dress, which was heavy, if not actually clumsy on her. She told him proudly told that she had made it herself. Like many women in Poland, he noticed she seemed to feel no desire to shave her legs, a lack which had taken a while to get used to, and he wondered with a wry smile whether there was a widespread shortage of female razors.

"Are you married?" she asked.

"No. And you?" he said quickly, hoping she had not seen his staring.

"Oh, no. I live with my parents and brother. Is England very good to live?" she asked eagerly, smiling and leaning towards him.

"Not now," answered John. "We have a lot of unemployment and a woman prime minister who doesn't seem to care for the poor."

"But that is their problem, John," said Ewelina briskly, shrugging her shoulders. "Britain is a place to do business, isn't it? We have no hope of that here."

"You have no unemployment here; in our country, it's almost 3 million. It's doubled since Thatcher came to power."

"But you are free, John. Free to make money. Free to do business." She tapped him on the knee. "Come. I want to dance."

Their dance was not like the one with Evonne One. In this loud music, Ewelina danced provocatively, her eyes flashing at him and her hands weaving an erotic pattern across her face. He wondered what to make of her and made an attempt to kiss her. She ducked under his arms, and when the music ended, she returned to where they had been sitting. The woman looked expectantly down at her empty glass. He picked it up, found out what she wanted to drink and went towards the bar, meeting Tim and their hosts on the way.

"Well, well, I see you are finding our nightlife to your taste, John?" quizzed Pavel, rolling a cigarette in his fingers before slowly bringing it to his mouth and inhaling. "What does she do for a living?"

"The same as me, a journalist," answered John quickly, before slipping off to the bar.

Pavel watched him go and turned to Tim with an amused expression.

"Do you know, the last time I was here I believe she said she was an engineer, just like me. I hope your friend doesn't make the mistake of falling in love with such as her."

John brought back the drinks and sat next to Ewelina who supped deeply on the cocktail. She thanked him and asked him if he was free to visit Wilanów Palace with her the following afternoon. They agreed to meet at the corner near the Hotel Bristol, which suited them to wait for a taxi.

Ewelina arrived late at the rendezvous, and he saw how plainly she was dressed, which made him feel that she was not working at the moment, or that most Poles were not affluent at all. He wondered whether to give her a peck on the cheek, but in the end, they simply shook hands and flagged down a taxi. The driver gave Ewelina an appreciative look up and down and asked which destination they wanted. He spoke in hesitant English to John as they drove towards the palace.

"Bad time now here. Too many queues. In my bar, I get to have only three bottles of beer each time go in. Then they say 'No'. Very, very bad."

"I'm sorry," said John. "If they did that in England, there'd be a revolution."

The taxi driver looked in the mirror at Ewelina and said in Polish: *"Are you hoping to get an English husband?"*

"I could do worse, and he is naive enough to be a catch," replied Ewelina, smiling.

"What if he hasn't got a lot of money?"

"I can take care of that if I can get there and marry him."

"What are you saying?" asked John.

"We are saying how the weather is not helping with the vegetables this year," replied Ewelina, taking his hand in hers and patting it. "That makes the queues and our faces grow longer."

John noticed the driver smiling and thought they were sharing a joke that must be common in Poland.

As they walked towards the impressive baroque building on an overcast, windy afternoon, Ewelina waltzed ahead of him and then spun suddenly around, smiling.

"You know why I am happy here? Not that just I am with a handsome English gentleman. By the way, do you think I am pretty?"

"I think you are attractive, yes," answered John, taken aback by her directness. "Do you?"

"I have regular features," she stated modestly, patting her cheeks. "No, the reason is I am happy because when this palace was being built it was a great, great time for Poland. Why? Because it was when we had an empire that ruled over many lands and peoples."

"And like any empire, exploited them?" suggested John, trying to keep pace with her.

"That is the way of all empires, especially your own," answered Ewelina, lifting her head and fixing her eyes on him. "We are different. Poles are not like other people. We have suffered very much but have kept our distinct ways and our beliefs. Our language and church. Imagine, John, if you had been occupied by Russians, Austrians and Germans and saw your Britain disappear. And then when we got our state back, along came the Nazis and destroy everything, even our whole city of Warsaw. What do you think that did to us? Then back came the Russians and made us communist slaves. What do you think that has done to us?"

"I suppose it has made you very insecure and wanting to hold on to what you have or what you think you can get," replied John, quietly.

John's musings were interrupted when he got a push from Tom and realised it was time to board. "Here beginneth the Great Adventure," he declared as they clambered up on to the coach with the others for the trip to Dover and the ferry to Ostend, getting a nod from his friend as they found a seat, greeting some of the other travellers.

The coach inched its way out of a busy but dreary London. John reached for something to read, but it was plain there was something that Tom wanted to get off his chest because he was constantly clearing his throat. His friend looked up from his book and said: "What's wrong?"

"Er, I just wanted to let you know that during that talk with my bosses, it became clear there was…er, maybe a threat to my person, so to speak."

"To your person?" echoed John, curious about this enigmatic line of conversation. "You mean the Bolsheviks are after you? They'll pounce at Minsk?"

"I have been reliably informed that they might be after my body."

"For medical research?"

"Let's just say that my bosses have warned me to be alert for any blondes who may try to force their favours on me."

"You mean you'll have no worries with their brunettes or redheads?" enquired John, who was instantly drowned out by his companion's tut-tutting.

"Look, I'll say this for the one and only time, John," began Tom, whispering in John's ear, his eyes for once wide open and alert. "Should there be any attempts at intimacy on our trip—"

"But I've…I've never fancied you, Tom."

"No!" Tom hissed. "I mean if we get approached, I want you to know I have brought something that will protect us."

"Does it have a silencer?"

"I have a number of packets of…er, protection…Should I remain unscathed, you're welcome to avail yourself of them. Let's face it, the blondes are more likely to make off with you than they are with me anyway."

"Thanks. But don't forget the redheads as well."

John saw a thin finger waving in his face and heard the warning words he had come to know so well. "Sometimes, Murphy, you *really* annoy me!"

Chapter Three

Not far from the ferry, which had berthed in Ostend, Louis was examining the papers handed to him by the latest batch of travellers, stifling a yawn.

This was going to be his twentieth coach journey to the Soviet Union and he and the driver had yet to have a break from what had become a chore. His mood was hardly helped by his relations with the coach driver who barely talked to him in a civil manner for most of the trip. He had got used to the travellers gravitating towards Arnaud with his winning smile. Neither did he resent his colleague's easy manner and his ability in finding female company during any trip.

Although he was younger by more than 10 years, Louis had a gauche way with him that was not usually associated with a Dutchman of his generation, unlike his Belgian colleague. Yet, he had a strong-looking face with attractive blue-grey eyes and thick blond hair, so it might have been expected that he would run Arnaud close in seducing any single women on the trips or married ones behind their husbands' backs. But Louis could not hide the fact that his interests lay in another direction and this made his relationship with the coach driver prickly on that count alone. During trips and for most of the time in the hotels, Louis would have his head buried in a book while Arnaud, after a long stint driving, would be in the bar chatting up the prettiest women on the coach or flirting with the girls serving the drinks.

Louis yearned for this trip to throw up someone he could get along with, but he surveyed with growing apathy, the group before him filing by with the usual 'Hellos' and grunts towards him. But what was this? He saw two men who looked an odd couple and tried to display a welcoming smile to both of them.

"Very good to meet you. I hope you enjoy the trip. You are…together?"

"We have asked for twin-bedded accommodation throughout," came the chilly response from the little one with heavy-rimmed glasses. Louis made his usual mental note to observe a discreet distance.

"If there's anything you might need to know, please don't hesitate to ask," he said keeping his smile with difficulty.

"Thanks. We're looking forward to what's to come," replied the little man's companion who appeared to the guide to be making a welcome effort to be sociable.

"We seem to have an interesting mix for the trip," said Louis. "Australians, Americans, English and all different ages, so I'm sure you'll find friends before too long."

"And you've been to the Soviet Union before?" asked John, who was amused when he saw Louis dramatically fling his hands upward.

"Oh, what haven't I seen there! Things that will surprise you and disappoint you. But you will see for yourself. Poland will be a surprise too."

"I know, I've been," replied John.

"And what did you find there?" asked Louis, warming to the unexpected conversation.

"A wife," answered Tom for John while his friend shrugged sheepishly.

Louis made another of his mental notes to observe a discreet distance and waved the two to where Arnaud was waiting to greet all the travellers.

The driver gave them a wave and took off his tinted spectacles, before shaking their hands. Arnaud was in his late thirties with shaggy dark hair and the first impression he made was that he was a man who was able to remain in control of most situations and listened to without having to raise his voice or become agitated. As far as this particular trip was concerned, he knew what to expect and what to be careful of, particularly when crossing into the Soviet Union and at the border with Finland where the frontier guards were convinced he was smuggling drugs. But after so many trips to what was not his favourite destination, he reckoned that he had learned all the tricks of the trade as a coach driver. There was the undoubted compensation of being the target of female attention as well as making sure the men were his pals.

"Welcome. I am your driver, Arnaud, and I want you to know that should you find during the journey that you need any nice, chilled Belgian beer, I have plenty of cans for a good price. And if you want any advice on where to go and what to see on the trip, come and ask me, *not* him," he added dismissively with a thumb over his shoulder in the direction of his colleague and snorting. "Unless you wanna go to the places *he* likes."

He grinned suggestively at John, but when his glance fell on Tom, he suddenly frowned.

"You, you are not…him?" he asked and then looked at John. "Is it him? Is he *the* one?"

"Depends if he wants to go to the same places as Louis," replied John.

"I most certainly am not the one," complained Tom, giving an enraged expression but relieved to see the coach driver nod in an agreement and wag a finger.

"No, you are not a movie star and not American. I mean, I thought: 'What is Woody Allen[10] doing on my coach without Annie Hall?' But my friend, you look so much like him…the height, those glasses. And look at the women he has. Wait till you get to Russia and get your teeth into the blondes. Or maybe they into you!"

Tom smacked his lips.

As he passed by and struggled up the coach steps, Arnaud looked back at John and declared under his breath, "I think my coach has a better chance of out-flying Concorde[11], don't you?"

"And now, ladies and gentlemen, on behalf of Astro Coach Tours, I would like to invite you to sit back and enjoy the surroundings as we drive away from Ostend to our first overnight destination of West Berlin where you will be free to have a wander around and see the night life. Our itinerary doesn't allow us to go into East Berlin, but we will have a drive around, and you will be able to see the landmarks of the Brandenburg Gate and of course, the Berlin Wall. All the history will be explained to you by our local guide.

"After that tour, we will drive the rest of the day, stopping off briefly in Poznan in Poland, until we get to the capital, Warsaw. Now, ladies and gentlemen, although Poland is a communist country, it is freer than the Soviet Union, despite the martial law. That was imposed in December 1981 and was only lifted last year. Our local guide there will be able to tell you more but don't be surprised if you see long queues outside the shops because they have rationing there. But you will be able to go where you want and take photos without any problem, and you will find maybe the young people will wanna chat with you. I have to warn you of one thing. There is a big black market for people who wanna change their currency, the zloty, for yours, especially if you have American dollars or West German Marks. Sterling is accepted but it's up to you.

Remember, you stay only a little while in Poland, and we don't come back through it. I'll tell you more on the way about the Soviet Union."

With that, Louis switched off the microphone and said a few words to Arnaud before opening his book and starting to read. From where he was sitting, John could see it was a novel by James Baldwin called *Giovanni's Room*[12]. There was no conversation between the courier and driver for a couple of hours and John and Tom looked out of the window and muttered a few words.

"Hey, are you guys English by any chance?"

The question came across the aisle from an elderly man with sunglasses and a full head of white hair who smiled at them and proffered his hand to shake with Tom.

"Been to your country many times, and it's got a lot going for it," said the man. "It's sure got even more now you got someone with balls running it. I see your Mrs Thatcher is gunning for the unions. She'll give the miners a good whipping. Yup, and she's got the right man with that boss Ian MacGregor[13] there to get them back down the mines again. He did great in the US bringing the miners to heel. Yup."

Tom and John exchanged glances, before looking back at the grinning American as he continued, "You've got a pretty cute dame in Maggie. And Ronnie back home just loves her."

"We don't think she's doing anything to help the poorest in our country," said John, coldly.

"My friend, what you've got to realise is that the poor have always been poor," started the American, "so, they've just got to learn to be poorer. Now, that's enough about politics, buddies, we're on vacation. We're going to be in this jalopy for a good few days, so might as well get the introductions done now. My name's Rick, Rick McCoy from Florida. Hey, little fellow, did anyone tell you how much you look like…?"

Chapter Four

The coach was making good progress along the autobahn to Berlin despite the rain, and it gave the travellers the opportunity to see the two Germanys both in motion and contrast.

Opals and Mercedes were gliding along the highway past chugging, two-stroke Trabants[14], some of which had to pull in to the hard shoulder when the rain got heavier. Passing the border from West to East Germany was the first indication of crossing the Iron Curtain with grim looking fortifications that stretched for miles. The second piece of evidence had been seeing these small vehicles with drivers hunched over the steering wheel.

Rick watched the Trabants and stopped chewing his gum.

"Jesus! Who'd be a commie driving a bucket like that?" he asked rhetorically, sipping on another can of beer from Arnaud's supply. "Even Fred Flintstone[15] could outspeed these jalopies, boys," he added, looking at Tom and John. "I'll tell you one thing; I didn't expect to stop being a capitalist on this trip, but if that's the best they can offer their own people, give me the bosses any time. Bet their leaders aren't squeezed into those tin cans. Hey, do you reckon their tanks are like that? They'd never win the arms race, not even if it was Sergeant Bilko[16] in charge on our side."

Tom turned to John and grimaced. Both shared a dislike of crowing Yanks they had met over the years but had suppressed views rather than start a row. But on this trip, they were going to be in contact with a strident and cocksure type that would be likely to brag about the superior American way of life till they got back to Ostend after two and a half weeks.

"You will not get into an argument," hissed Tom to John. "Promise me you won't."

"Expect me to keep quiet with all that?" replied John. "The bloke's obnoxious. Why shouldn't he be challenged? *Why?*"

"Because it's unseemly," declared Tom, sipping on another of Arnaud's tins, "and I refuse to be drawn into any contretemps on my holiday. You know I'm already under pressure at work about this break. I just want to have a relaxing time."

Tom completed his statement with a sweep of his hand and nod of his head that showed he would brook no dissent, and John realised it was futile to disagree, followed by his friend insisting: "Now, that's my final word. I'll have that other tin, please."

"Hey, Woody, your latest film, that *Broadway Danny Rose* got you back in my good books."

Tom looked impassively at Rick and muttered: "I beg your pardon?"

"Sure, it made me laugh, not like that one last year. *Zelig* sucked as far as I was concerned. Too clever by half. You can do better than that, Woody, even though you're screwin' Mia Farrow. I bet when you did, you sung her ex's *I Did It My Way.*"

John watched with mounting concern when he saw Tom swing around and face Rick.

"My name is not Woody. My name is Thomas."

"Well, it sure ain't Spartacus, little fellah," agreed Rick, raising his can to Tom.

Before John could do anything, Tom had knocked Rick's can from his hand, which went flying and hit a dozing Australian tourist behind them who felt his forehead and declared: "Jeez! How did a 'Roo get in here?"

There was then the sight of the elderly American grappling on the floor with the English public servant, leading to pandemonium in the coach as it quickly pulled over to the hard shoulder. Arnaud came hurriedly back and separated the two, a hand on both as he led them off the coach, followed by Louis and John.

"What the hell are you people doing?" demanded Arnaud, looking at the two unlikely fighters in front of him.

"This little runt needs a good hiding!" growled Rick, which prompted Tom to raise his fists.

John looked around him and saw not only the coach travellers watching the action with a mixture of bemusement and mirth but the many Trabant drivers and passengers also giggling at the lanky Yank and the diminutive civil servant squaring up to one another. To add to that, an East German police car had arrived quietly and two policemen got out and watched the scene playing out before them.

"Oh, putting up your dukes to me, are you?" said Rick with his hands on hips and sneer playing on his lips. "I was in the marines, Limey. I blew away the Chinks in Korea so I sure can do that with you." At that, Rick grabbed hold of Tom's jacket lapels and lifted him off the ground, his feet doing a running motion and causing more laughter in the coach.

"Please, what is going on here?" The polite question from one of the policemen caused the four to look around.

"Oh, Christ," whispered Arnaud to Louis. "Welcome to the fucking GDR."

Louis advanced towards the policemen, still with his novel in hand and an awkward smile playing on his lips.

"We are very, very sorry. I think the gentlemen here were having a little disagreement that got, er, out of hand. They have resolved their differences, haven't you?" Louis asked Rick and Tom, earnestly.

"I do not understand why the tall man there grabbed the little man here, if that is so," commented the policeman, approaching the two. "Your passports, please."

Flicking through them, a frown appeared on the policeman's face as he handed them back.

"So, you are an American and you are British and you are fighting when I thought you were allies."

"You call that fighting, buddy?" quizzed Rick, cocking his thumb at Tom who glowered back. "I've had a tougher fight with a Chink corpse than with this guy."

The policeman came closer to Tom and looked him up and down. "If I had not seen your passport, sir, I would have said that you look just like—"

"Spartacus?" hinted Rick. "Before or after he was crucified?"

Tom bristled and clenched his fists, and it seemed as if he was ready to launch an ill-advised attack, which led Arnaud to come between them and grab hold of both their right hands.

"Gentlemen, gentlemen, we have a destination to get to this evening and Berlin awaits. Now, I'm sure the policemen here will be delighted to see you shake hands, and we'll be on our way. I know I will and I have all these people on board who think the same."

The coach driver's grip on both their hands was as insistent as his look, and Tom and Rick reluctantly shook hands, mumbled a few words and made their way back to the coach. While they did so, the policemen acknowledged Arnaud's relieved smile and nod of the head. But the English speaking policeman stopped Louis and asked to see his book, flicking through the pages, pretending not to see the Dutchman's increasing concern.

"This book is about? *Giovanni's Room*. It's by that American black activist who loves men."

"Er, the novel's about a friendship in Paris."

"Romantic?"

"Some might think so."

"I think so too; I have read it. No problems, safe trip to Berlin," concluded the policeman, smiling at the timid Louis and saluting. "But make sure those two allies don't go to war again on GDR territory."

While the dispute was being carried out, John shut his eyes and started to recall another farce back in Christmas 1981. He was watching the television and the news bulletin had made it clear that the Solidarity[17] leaders had not been executed but had all been rounded up, while the reports of a number of supporters being killed were verified.

He had observed the coverage with mixed emotions. What had the Poles expected surrounded by Warsaw Pact[18] countries and treating the regime as if they were ruling the roost now? Yes, Polish Pope John Paul II[19] had condemned the move as had the Western leaders but hadn't they realised what had happened in 1968 in Czechoslovakia[20]? The Polish regime had dealt harshly with unrest before as they had shown in the workers' riot in Gdansk two years later after the Czechoslovak suppression.

The young Poles he had met in London appeared not to appreciate their country tiptoeing to a disaster with claims that Lech Wałęsa[21] was destined to form a government in the New Year.

"John, the communists are finished; they can do nothing without Solidarity," said a young blonde, dancing closely with him at a disco underneath the Polish Society in South Kensington. "Do you know we have no cream in Poland, no basics? Things must change. By the way, do you know any British friends who would like to marry for convenience for good money? Are *you* married?"

John poured some more beer into his glass and heard the phone sound. He rose slowly and picked up the receiver.

"Hello?"

"John? John?" came the familiar voice. "John, this is Ewelina."

"I know," he answered, brushing his hair back and sighing. "How was your Christmas?"

"It was terrible," he heard her reply. "Terrible, there is civil war in Poland."

"Perhaps not that bad…"

"…You know nothing; I speak to my family."

"And the rest of the Christmas?"

"It was a disaster in the hotel."

"You still work there in Earl's Court?"

"Yes, after we split up, they asked me to stay and work there and move in. There was an Arab man; he was a guest. He was like a father to me."

"Not a sugar daddy?"

"What? I don't understand you. Please do not joke; I always hated when you did that after we married."

"What happened to this man?"

"We had a party with some of the guests and staff, and we danced and had good time."

"Sounds very enjoyable."

"But you remember how I danced?"

"Very difficult to forget."

"My wild eyes and you know the rest. Well, it was too much for the poor man and he had a heart attack and dropped dead."

"*What?*"

"In front of me at one moment he was standing and dancing a bit, saying the plans he had for me, then next on the floor, dead, very dead, completely dead."

"But what happened next? Did you call an ambulance?"

"We have so many illegal workers in the hotel we decided to take him up to his room covered in a blanket and put him to bed after we got him in his pyjamas. He had very nice silk ones, you know. And how are you, John?"

"Just about recovering. You know I was under 10 stone in weight and going grey when we split up two months after we married."

"That's your problem, John."

"Why, when you ask me and I tell you how bad I was, you tell me it's my problem?"

"Because it is and my problems are more than yours. I am alone and my father and brother are in Warsaw with bloody martial law there. What is to become of them?"

"Haven't you forgotten one person in all this that you should care about?"

"I cannot care for you because you do not look after me, John, not from the day we married."

"I tried to care for you, Ewelina. It wasn't me I was thinking about caring for."

"All I know is that I can only care about me, only me."

"What about the son you left behind in Warsaw that you didn't tell me about from your first marriage?"

"Oh, I will take him when the time is right. John; it wasn't business for me to tell you about that marriage and child. But I want to tell you this. I have regrets about you and me, yes, I have."

"You told people in the hotel that I tried to change your religion and get you into prostitution."

"So, I regret my exaggeration. You must understand I had not returned in my mind; I was crazy for a while…There was something wrong with my heart. So, I say to you now that I am prepared to have you back, and we can be happy, and you can help me get the British nationality."

"There are a couple of things that have played on my mind in the time we were together."

"I'm ready to answer all your questions. We need have no secrets. We're still husband and wife."

"You never explained why you didn't return to me the day after our wedding and no one in the hotel would say where you were. When you came back, there was a mark on your chest, like a bite. Tell me…"

"…Silly John, it was a misunderstanding. I was elsewhere, that's all for you to need to know. Yes and the bite…No, it was like a bruise, just a bruise. You have only to trust me."

"And why did you ask if I considered whether you were unfaithful if you had a lesbian affair?"

"It was what do you call it? It was a rhetorical question."

"Do you realise how angry all of this has made me? I can't believe how arrogant you are."

"Yes, some people find me like that. But some people find me nice; some people find me beautiful."

"Oh, I know you find yourself beautiful…"

"…Stop, stop. The main thing for you to know is the good news that I have returned in my mind now, so forget all that. We can go to Paris and Rome next year. Yes, I am prepared to have you back, John."

"Over my dead body, Ewelina."

"You are a fool, John. You were always jealous of me because compared with me, you are very ordinary. So *very* ordinary. You know what I ask myself all the time? *Dlaczego musiałem poślubić takiego spastyka?*" (Why did I have to marry such a spastic?)

"I can guess what the last word means. But like I said, over my dead, *spastic* body. Do you know why? Unlike your sugar daddy, I'm a live one, Ewelina."

Tom and Rick went around the coach apologising profusely for their indiscretion and most of the travellers took it in good stead, and they returned quietly to their seats, shaking hands again with one another.

Rick raised Tom's arm as high as he could and declared, "Hey, guys, I taught Muhammad Ali everything he knew but this fellah does a shuffle to die for!"

Despite the bonhomie, John decided that it might be better to be a buffer and sat in Tom's place while they listened to Arnaud's ironical voice over the system.

"Hello, ladies and gentlemen. Please forgive the unannounced comfort break back there. Our arrival time in Berlin will be slightly later than planned but early enough for you to have a nice dinner wherever you want. Now just relax…*all* of you!"

A ripple of laughter and applause went through the coach as they settled back for the rest of the trip to Berlin, and it gave John the time to take out a slip of paper with an address to consider.

"Are you going ahead with the idea of making contact with her family?"

He looked at Tom and smiled awkwardly at the question.

"How are you going to get anything across if they don't speak English?"

"I'm hoping the local guide there will come and translate."

He saw Tom considering what to say next, but he thought again and remained silent.

"I want to explain to them that I tried my best with Ewelina and…"

Seeing his friend give a shrug of the shoulders and start reading a book, John stopped his explanation. He looked down again at the scrap of paper with the address and telephone number that he had hurriedly scrawled from her diary and kept for the chance that one day he would be in Warsaw.

Chapter Five

Tom shifted uneasily on his seat in the nondescript hotel restaurant/bar as the two Australian girls on the other side of the table observed him and exchanged glances.

The group had checked in, and he was waiting for John to bring back the beer from the bar. Tom found the attention was unsettling and wondered what he could say to get the ball rolling with them as he was still finding the drink on the coach had made him feel less inhibited. The girls were cousins and in their early twenties. One was quite good looking with sparkling brown eyes and very comely legs that he had confessed to his friend always attracted him.

"I suppose you're a breast man?" he once said to John when they were in an Irish nightclub, eyeing up the talent that once the lights went up, tended to scare, rather than enthral.

"No, I'm a 'Thankful that you're even interested in me' man," replied John.

"Are you always scrapping, mate?" asked the good-looking girl to Tom. "I took you for more of a koala than a croc."

"Joan, don't tease the man," scolded the plain-looking one.

"Well, I can't help it. I thought this coach trip would be boring; Jane and this fellow and the Yank popped up and gave it some fizz. So, do you break up the chairs in your local bar?"

"Er, only when riled," mumbled Tom, warming to the apparent appreciation society that had formed. "My name's Thom…Tommy," he stuttered, plumping for getting the relationship on an informal footing.

"You mean, like the Pinball Wizard?" exclaimed Joan, her beautiful hazel eyes growing wider.

"Well, um, I suppose if I took off my glasses I would be similarly afflicted," confessed Tom, removing his spectacles. "But, er, I'm not deaf or dumb…as you can see. *Hah*!"

The two girls tittered, which made Tom feel even better as he put on his glasses and repeated: "*Hah!*"

He looked around for John and saw him at the bar, still waiting to be served and decided to help with the beer and smiled at his fan club.

"Please don't worry, I will return," he assured them with a smack of his lips.

"Don't be long, Tommy," pleaded Joan, looking down at her almost empty glass that she nudged towards him. Tom gave a tap on his nose and pointed at the glasses and nodded.

"I'll be back in a jot with suitable replenishments."

John was ordering the round when Tom came up and tugged at his jacket.

"Good news, I've pulled," he blurted out, causing the bartender to pause in pouring the beer and give an oblique glance at the excited little man.

"What? How? Where?" replied a disbelieving John.

"The two Australian girls back there were impressed with my tackling Rick, and honestly, John, they could be our conquests for tonight." The bartender apologised for spilling the beer and started again. "Could you get them beer as well? I'll pay, yes. I'll pay."

Tom's insistence was such that John agreed and followed his friend who was spilling the contents in his eagerness to return to resume his success. He almost bumped into Tom as his companion halted suddenly. There before them opposite the two women was a big, strapping man who had spread himself on his side, making it impossible for anyone else to sit with him. The same age and nationality as the girls, he was assured with tanned skin and muscles everywhere that could be imagined. He sipped his drink casually, occasionally running his fingers through his thick, curly blond hair, which led Tom to suffer more than usual from his inferiority complex.

"I brought you your drink," mumbled Tom and placed them down, waiting for a sign of appreciation.

"Yeah, great...Now, what were you saying about Bali, Pip? I'd so love to go there," exclaimed Joan, fluttering her thick, luscious eyelashes. "And you're from Perth as well."

"Yeah, live in Alfred Cove. You must come and look me up."

"Oh, don't worry; we will. But getting back to Bali, it's right top of the list for me to go."

"It's mine too!" echoed Jane, leaning forward, taking the glass of beer Tom had brought without acknowledging him and sipping deeply.

"I…I was sitting there," interrupted Tom, pointing to where Pip was sitting.

Pip looked at Tom from head to foot and smiled with predictably perfect, gleaming white teeth and glanced around him.

"Couple of spaces over there, guys," he responded, waving graciously to the opposite end of the bar. "Ladies, now let me tell you about Bali. The beaches, nightlife. Say, how about going there next year, but we'll speak about that on this trip…"

Tom and John sloped away. As he came by his friend and looked down, John could see that even with his impassive expression, there was hurt pride within Tom wanting to surface but which was characteristically being suppressed.

"I thought they were interested in me, but I can see they were just a couple of tarts," stated Tom forlornly.

"They're young and found someone like them, Tom. You're a yet to be naked civil servant, and I'm a sozzled, ageing hack. Wait till we bump into those Russian blondes."

The two sat down and drank sombrely, occasionally watching the strides Perth Pip was making with the young women. They had not noticed that Rick had witnessed the whole business and was behind them, enjoying their mulling.

"The trouble with you mugs is you lack the confidence he has," he declared and saw them spin around. "Look at me. I'm old enough to be your pa, but I bet you I could have laid one of them dames before the trip had ended. Okay, okay, I can see the look in your eyes. I'm just a bragging Yank who waves his dollars and the pussy comes a'running. You don't need no money, guys, just confidence and a way to tickle their fancy to make 'em relax. The rest is job done. Sure I go with the toms to relieve myself from time to time but then some will give me a pensioner discount, you know what I mean? Hey, do they have toms in the Eastern Bloc?"

Rick watched as he saw Tom give a disconsolate nod of his head and sink the rest of the beer. After the shaky start, the American was beginning to warm to this peculiar man. He was no therapist, but he could see the Englishman was extremely repressed and wanted desperately to somehow rid himself of the image of a boring person.

"Hey, Woo…Thomas, how's about me and you go and paint the town redder than it is in East Berlin? What do you say? I hear this part of the city is full of go-go bars. If we're lucky, there might be some come-come bars too."

"I really feel that your offer is not for me," answered Tom, shaking his head confidently.

The girls were dancing and their hips revolved erotically as they felt and kissed one another's bare breasts and looked out, blinded by the garish spotlight, just about picking out two silhouettes in the rows before them.

Tom and Rick sat in the front where they had been guided by a beefy, bouncer who assured them that the show was about to really take off. The dancers looked very bored and one barely stifled a yawn while Rick assured his companion that the night was young. Tom hoped so but was regretting he had not stayed in the hotel with John. However, the sight of Pip walking to the bar with Joan on his arm had been the deciding factor in agreeing to join the American on a trip around the Berlin dives.

It started off well enough as the first stop was a loud bar where US army personnel was present and seemed to take to him warmly until they realised he was not 'the' famous film director. Even Rick found the raucous laughter and behaviour were getting too much for him, and he had suggested to Tom it was time to go native. They wandered till they found a bar off the main street and tried out their German on a grim looking *frau* who was oblivious to any attempt by Rick to respond with a smile.

"I wanted to say about this afternoon when we had our set to," began Rick to Tom. "I know my mouth gets a bit outta control, so apologies."

"I really think I should—"

"No, Tom, I'm at an age now when no words can be better than too many. Now, that's hard for a man who's been selling second hand cars for most of his life to say. Oh, and what do you do?"

Tom cleared his throat and told Rick his job and noted a roll of the eyes by his companion.

"You mean you have two trays on the desk where paper has to be moved from one to the other *every* day?"

"I may be a bureaucrat, Rick, but I have worked on very important issues," replied Tom, finding his temper beginning to rise.

"Such as, pal?"

"I really don't think we have reached the status of pals, do you?" stated a clearly miffed Tom.

"Okay," acknowledged Rick, amused by the Englishman's growing agitation. "So, just which size of paper clips are you responsible for ordering?"

"It might interest you to know that I once worked in Northern Ireland fighting against the IRA!"

The statement caused Rick to raise his eyebrows, and he let out a high whistle as he moved back a little and surveyed Tom better.

"Whoa! And how many republicans did you bag in your time?"

"Mine was a battle of…the mind, not, er, of the body," muttered Tom. "I didn't physically fight, that was the army's role. I'd like to know if you ever supported Northern Ireland. I doubt you'd know where to find it on the map."

"Oh, I give support, buddy, but to a body that really helps the people over there. NORAID[22]."

When he finished the sentence, Tom could barely contain his rage and slipped off the stool and banged his fists on the bar counter.

"NORAID? NORAID? That bloody front to the IRA?"

"What's your problem? How'd you reckon we kicked the British asses out of the colonies…egg and spoon races?"

The two squared up again with Rick towering over his opponent and Tom adopting a classical pugilistic stance. The bar had fallen silent already and the few that were there were looking amazed at one another at the sight of the foreigners appearing ready to land blows.

"Halt! Halt!" screamed the woman behind the bar. "Are you two mad?" she added, rushing out from the bar and coming between them. "Ve have quiet bar and you two vant to fight? *Here*?"

"It won't take long, sweetheart," promised Rick. "One tap on his chin and he'll fold."

"*Nein*! *Nein*! You horrible big Yankee bully. This little man, leave alone."

"Oh, I get it, honey. You Krauts were always ones for the little guys like Goebbels and the Führer, weren't you?" accused Rick, putting an arm around Tom's shoulder and guiding him towards the front door. He turned imperiously around and glowered at the woman. "I promise you this; we will never darken your doorway again! Come on, Adolf, we'll find another place where we'll be welcome. How far is Stalingrad from here, old buddy?"

The rapprochement had continued after they left, and within a few yards, they were on talking terms again with Rick using all the persuasive skills he had built up over the years, allied to Tom's increasing drunkenness. So, they had ended in this bar with the girls dancing away before them with one trying particularly hard to get a reaction of any kind from Tom, coming closer to him, raising her index finger and devouring it in her mouth.

"She'll make herself ill," he whispered into Rick's ear and then said to her, "I say, be careful, you'll choke on your digit...*Hah!*"

Before he knew it, the girl had jumped down from the stage and was sitting with her arm around him, stroking his neck, while the other one did the same with Rick. The American smiled and laughed at this, but Tom was rigid with apprehension as the beads of sweat started trickling down his forehead.

"*Bist du Deutscher, schatz? Es-tu français, mon cher?*" enquired the girl, who now put her arm around Tom's shoulder.

"E-E-English, actually," stammered Tom.

"How nice. My name is Julia. And your name is?"

"T-T-Thomas."

"I like you, T-T-Thomas," purred Julia, tickling his chin. "I like you very much. You are not like other men," she continued, observing the sweat pouring down his forehead. "No, not like any other men at all."

Thomas kept his eyes ahead of him as he felt her plump, naked breast on his arm. If only Joan in the hotel had shown a similar eagerness to get to know him. If only he had the way to let himself relax in their presence and they in his. He was now aware of Julia's hand travelling down to his hip, knee and along his thigh accompanied on his side by a spurt but only in perspiration. He looked beyond the stage and saw a narrow walkway with cubicles on both sides and black curtains on each. It intrigued him and while Julia's tongue was somehow probing his inner ear he asked:

"What are those places?"

"They are...rest rooms, dear T-T-Thomas. Perhaps you are feeling tired. Have you come far today?"

"From London, actually. I think maybe I should leave and go to bed," he stated beginning to rise with difficulty but finding that Julia's hand pressed firmly on his chest quickly returned him to his seat.

"Oh, no, there's no need. For a little deposit, you can stay here in one of our rest rooms. I can offer you some comforting massage and drink. I am a trained masseuse, and you look like someone who needs to have his problems eased away. You have problems with your work?" Tom nodded his head. "Your wife?" Tom shook his head. "Your lover?" Tom shook his head vigorously. "Let me help you forget any problems for only 200 Marks."

"But that's £50!" exclaimed Tom.

"Look deeply into my eyes, dear man," began Julia slowly. "I see you are not at peace with yourself. Let me soothe you with this, and I promise your troubles will fade…fade…*fade*."

Her beguiling, reassuring words began to affect him, along with the beer he had consumed that day, and he was convinced her eyes were penetrating into his mind. They were so clear and blue even though the whites were rather bloodshot. He reached for his wallet and handed over 200 Marks and smiled rather childishly back at her but seemed only to see those deep azure, now sparkling eyes. His own began to droop as she took his hand and led him towards one of the cubicles, without him gazing down to see an amused Rick watching his journey to disappearing behind the curtain.

"Perhaps you too would like to rest, darling?" whispered his companion into his ear. "I have always preferred the older, experienced man. He knows how to give pleasure to the younger woman."

"Oh, I do, honey, but I'm just starting the holiday, and well, you're looking at a pensioner here."

The girl pouted her lips and stroked his nose and chin.

"And you Americans are always my favourite nation."

"Now, if I were a Frenchman, what's the betting you'd say that?" asked a cynical Rick, patting her arm.

"Oh, no, darling. The French and Italian men are very much like they are the kings. You Americans are saving us from the communists. You are the heroes of the Free World and I am so grateful to you for keeping us so."

"And you mean to say we American men are quiet and modest?"

"Oh, yes and to show I am honest, I can give you a concessionary pensioner rate. I haven't told you my name is Shirley, named after your great Hollywood star, Shirley Temple. My dearest…?"

"Rick."

"Oh, my dearest Rick, I would like very much to travel up and down on your *Good Ship Lollipop* and…"

Before she could go further, they heard an uproar from the cubicle where Tom had disappeared with Julia, and he emerged suddenly, his shirt open, trousers and pants about his knees but carrying his shoes. His eyes no longer drooped but neither did his organ, which had a condom precariously placed on the end.

"Massage? Massage?" he bellowed with terrified and bulging eyes, hauling up his trousers and pants and scurrying to the exit where the big bouncer blocked him.

"*Hat er dich bezahlt?*" he demanded of Julia.

"Yes, he has paid."

The barman opened the door to let the fleeing Tom pass, bowed and said politely in English: "Goodbye. Please come again soon, sir."

John was waiting in the coach with the other travellers, hoping that there would be no further delay in the city tour.

He had decided to have a quiet drink in the hotel bar before heading to bed, fully expecting his friend to be back before long, especially as he was with someone who was so unlike him as Rick. But the hours passed by, and it was about 4am before he heard the room door flung open and the light switched on and then as quickly switched off.

"Sorry, sorry," he heard Tom mutter. "Sorry, sorry."

"Where the hell have you been?"

"I'd rather wait till the morning before I say where."

"It is the bloody morning, Tom!"

"Er, sorry, sorry."

John had turned over, swearing to himself as it was unlikely that he would get anything but apologies from Tom. Still fuming a few hours later, he had got up and ruefully observed the slumbering friend and went to shower and pack his clothes in the suitcase before heading with it to breakfast, giving Tom a shove and telling him to do the same. He heard a few muffled words of agreement and some movement that made him believe that he would be joined later by Tom with the group.

But here he was, apologising to the others, including two very irate elderly Australian ladies who were aunts of the young girls in the bar that had spurned them for Pip.

"Jeez, where's yer mate?"

"We'd never take him for one to be shagging the sheilas at this time of day," commented the other bluntly who made Dame Edna Everage look feminine. "Is he with the Yank too?"

"I'm here, good lady," stated Rick.

They turned around and saw the American looking fresh faced and spritely as he moved to his seat and nodded to all in the coach. When he saw John, he gave a slight wink and chuckled.

"Woody's one for livening up the evenings. I've not seen a sight like that in all my years."

"Where is the bugger?" muttered John through extremely gritted teeth.

"Why I do believe I see some little chap struggling to the coach," observed Rick.

The coach group greeted Tom with stony silence and damning stares as he found his way to John, sitting subdued and hunched, holding a hand over his face and shaking his head, whispering: "I'm so ashamed, John. We went to a nightclub and all I can say is that things got fuzzy, and I ended up in the road half-naked, clutching at my…my…clothes."

"Oh, Christ, as long as no one else saw this happen," hissed John.

"Good morning, ladies and gentlemen, this is Louis, hoping that you had a good night. I know someone in our party did when I was passing the *Little Pinkie* nightclub, but my lips are sealed! Let me introduce you to our local guide for the Berlin city tour. Here is Helga."

Louis passed the microphone to a young and serious woman in her mid-thirties who, despite the overcast morning, wore tinted glasses. She surveyed the group for a moment and then cleared her throat.

"Thank you, Louis, and hello to you all. Berlin is my birthplace, ladies and gentlemen, and I have to tell you a great irony about my birth. You see, I was born on 7 October 1949, the same day that the German Democratic Republic was founded by that nice man in Moscow, Joseph Stalin. So, what does that tell you? It tells you we have a city that has a story of grandeur and tragedy and today of division…

"And now, as we travel, you will see the Brandenburg Gate, built in the eighteenth century but today symbolising so graphically the division of the German people. You can see the Soviet soldiers strutting around in front of it as if it is their own. Ah, one waves to you; perhaps, it is the hand of friendship, or do I see a clenched fist?

"You know, in the Battle of Berlin, a third of it was smashed to smithereens by the Red Army, and I have to say that many German women were despoiled by the Russians. When I say 'despoiled', I mean raped. They were aged from before puberty to those who were grandmothers. Gang raped and then butchered.

Do you know what Uncle Joe in Moscow told Churchill and others? 'Let the boys have some fun.'

"Afterwards, the infrastructure, the railways and industry were dismantled and taken by them to their country…

"Here is another symbol of our tragic past, ladies and gentlemen, the Reichstag, our parliament building that was destroyed by the advancing Russian hordes, I mean liberators. It has been rebuilt but without the glories of much of its architecture and is a place for minor events for my home city. Berlin has a so-called parliament in the GDR part while the free parliament is in Bonn…

"And now we come to our final stop, ladies and gentlemen, to the symbol of the triumph of socialism, the Berlin Wall. Our comrades over there call it the Anti-Fascist Wall, and it was built in 1961 but do you notice something? Do you see? There are two walls and in between is a no-man's land with all the facilities aimed not at stopping people getting in but to prevent those escaping, ladies and gentlemen. Up until August 1961, millions left the socialist paradise but the Wall and the other fortifications stopped that and for those considered proletarian traitors, barbed wire, dogs and machine guns showed them there was – as they would term it – a better way. Yes, a better way. We stopped by the Wall, ladies and gentlemen so that you can observe there a guard post opposite with soldiers of the GDR. They are observing you too, and they make sure the no-man's land is not cluttered with any human remains for too long. The last death was of Silvio Proksch who was shot in the back on Christmas Day last year. Yes, ladies and gentlemen, the day of peace and goodwill to all mankind. Is it not kind that this year, 1984, the gentle soldiers of the GDR have had no rifle practice? Perhaps you would like to show your appreciation and greet them now?"

John watched in disbelief as the coach party roared and hurled abuse and gestured at the guard post with even Tom rushing to the side of the coach facing the graffiti decorated wall and alongside Rick, displayed a two-fingered greeting.

"Oh, God, Karl, it's the next bunch of western tourists."

"I wouldn't mind, but they are so rude with their gestures to us, Uwe."

"Look at that little one with the big glasses. My God, he looks like Comrade Erich Honecker[23]! Has he defected?"

"No such luck."

"Shush!"

Chapter Six

The group calmed down as they got out of the coach to stretch and chat in front of the wall with a number gathering around Helga.

John looked at the Berlin Wall and felt an enormous depression hitting him. It had such an air of permanence, and despite the colourful and in places, imaginative graffiti on this side, it barely hid a tale of bloodshed and frustration that was dominated, most of all, by a sense of futility. It struck him harder than all the damning words the local guide had mentioned in her commentary.

In recent years, the individuals and groups who had defended the Cold War status quo in favour of the Soviet bloc were dwindling back in Britain despite the ratcheting up of the stakes.

One exception he remembered was when he spoke four years before to a South African communist in London who insisted that the Wall had been there before the Second World War. And as far as the invasion of Czechoslovakia was concerned, she declared there were more CIA agents than Soviet soldiers in the country in 1968.

"Oh, come on, you're not in my bed to talk about military manoeuvres," she insisted, and he had nodded and waved his white flag in what was already a drunken, loveless night.

Now he was standing in front of this structure and what did he see? People strolling by themselves or as couples and families, who had grown used to its presence. He paused to see a child tracing her finger along the painting of a massive purple flower. She giggled and danced a little in front of her mother before running along to the next part of the painted wall, looking back at her parent and waving to be joined. Would she be painting her own flowers there in a few years' time while the GDR guards watched the latest batch of gesticulating tourists swearing at them? How could it be any different?

The little girl continued her dancing down the wall and to John's astonishment, stopped at what seemed like a garden right by it. He followed her and the mother and came to it, looking baffled by this contrast. Here was a site of growing sunflowers and vegetable areas brushing against this structure.

The mother looked at him with some amusement when he inadvertently expressed some astonished words in English as he gazed at the sight before him.

"It makes you wonder?" she asked in good English. "An old Turkish gentleman decided to do something with this space. It is technically a part of the GDR, but they went and built the wall in a straight line. The residents here just threw their rubbish here and Herr Kalin said: 'What a terrible waste.' You see, as he was a pensioner, he had the time, and he cleared the space and grew the vegetables and built this little hut."

"But didn't the authorities object?" asked John.

"Yes, yes, on both sides, but he told them to get lost. He was very angry with the West Berlin police most of all. The GDR guards came to check on him to see if he was building a tunnel but saw he wasn't, and he gave them some onions and garlic. Last Christmas, they sent him a bottle of wine even though he's a Muslim and doesn't drink. You see, there is some humanity in all of us when we try. There he is!"

John followed her pointing and sure enough, sitting by the Berlin Wall was an elderly man, leaning back on a rickety chair and smiling at all around him. He had a full, greying beard and a skullcap but wore cheap, western clothes. His sparkling eyes looked at him, and he nodded towards the Englishman and spread his arms as if to show that no matter what the silly officials might say, this little area was his.

John thanked the woman and walked back slowly to the group with a little faith restored in what could be achieved. But now, he was before Helga, and he tried to see past those tinted glasses and discover how pleased she was by what she had managed in the coach.

"Do you always get such a response from coach parties?" he asked.

"They often become agitated when they hear the truth, yes," she answered. "I think you won't get this from your Intourist guide when you travel in the workers' Shangri-La."

She nodded and walked away from him and made her way through the tourists who muttered their thanks for her talk.

"She knows how to whip up a crowd," John declared to a sheepish Tom. "I haven't seen you more stirred since England last beat the West Indies."

"Did I know you then?"

"Come to think of it, did your mother?"

"I suppose I could have been more circumspect," agreed Tom, watching Helga stride into the distance, "but she did have some points even you, *even you*, must agree with that, Murphy."

Before John could answer, Louis called the group to get into the coach for the 500-km journey to Warsaw. Arnaud gave Tom a very long, amused look, nodding knowingly to John: "I've been on this trip many times and something tells me the best is yet to come. By the way, *Małe Pinkie* is Polish for guess what in case your friend desires a similar nightclub."

The trip to Poland began with the experience of having to go through a frontier crossing between West Berlin and the GDR to get on the highway to Warsaw with a request that all passports be handed over to Louis who took them to the checkpoint to be inspected.

He returned with a severe-looking and expressionless woman frontier guard who climbed up and inspected the group before walking down the aisle.

"Why, good morning," said Rick, smiling sweetly and peeling a banana.

"Good morning," she replied, looking down at the American and how he slowly munched on the fruit.

"Bananas are so delicious and plentiful in *that* part of Berlin," he said, pointing with his thumb to the rear of the coach. "I've got a small bunch here if you'd like some."

"We have…no need…we have our own…alternatives," she answered in staccato fashion.

"Really? Are they black, bruised *and* pickled?"

The comment made her face contort, and she glared at Rick, turned her back momentarily and then shouted: "You will come with me and bring those bananas with you!"

"Oh, honey, you can take a joke, can't you?" said Rick, standing despairingly, looking around him and seeing a wall of sullen travellers staring back. "Apologies, folks," he began, holding up the banana skin in one hand and a bag of unpeeled bananas, the guard had demanded, in the other. "Seems I slipped up on this one."

As he passed by one of the English travellers, Rick heard him remark sharply: "Bloody lucky you didn't say you've got a lovely bunch of coconuts too!"

The room Rick was ushered into was threadbare with a plain table and two chairs and a manual 'Erika' typewriter in the centre with two piles of paper on either side. Facing him and surrounded by faded flock wallpaper hung a pale-coloured portrait of a man with heavy glasses, tightly drawn skin and receding hairline. The man's head was slightly tilted and his gaze was quizzical with just a hint that a smile might be playing on his thin lips. Rick blinked a few times.

"Woody?" he exclaimed, pointing at the framed photograph.

"I don't understand you," replied the woman, coldly. "I see no wood. That is our honourable leader, Comrade Erich Honecker."

Rick nodded and placed the bag with the bananas on the table and faced her.

"Now, sweetheart, I can't be long because those people on the coach will be even more angry with me if we're delayed getting to Warsaw."

The woman went behind the table and pulled out the chair, shaking her head.

"It isn't as easy as that."

"Oh, baby, why not?" pleaded Rick, sitting down on the other chair as she remained standing.

"It is my belief that you are involved with illicit trade."

His eyes widened, and he hit his hand on his forehead, too amazed to speak.

"For all that's holy, what?" he eventually spluttered.

"Those," she answered, pointing to the bag.

"You…you mean…bananas?"

"It may surprise you to know there is a black market in this produce in the GDR due to…unforeseen import difficulties. This illegal profiteering cannot be tolerated, and I am commandeering them."

She reached across and took the bag, bringing it close to her and opening it. Her eyes grew wider and softened, and he watched as her tongue barely peeped out of her mouth and went around her lips. It was a moment that seemed like a naughty child who had been left alone in a sweet shop and had not been allowed in for a long time. The guard suddenly looked at Rick and cleared her throat.

"You will, of course, get a receipt for this with a stamp."

"You're giving me a stamp for illicit goods?" he queried.

"I will type this out and stamp it. If you make any more comments, you and your coach party will be surprised how slowly I can type. Sometimes I have even been known to go into reverse."

There was no point asking the person behind the table with a severe face if she could be joking, and Rick watched as she got two A4 papers and slipped a carbon sheet between them and banged away carefully on the manual typewriter. She asked tersely what his full name was, and he responded flatly while she completed the typing, almost ripped out the papers and then stamped the top one. She signed it and ordered him to do the same.

"Er, I suppose they will be taken away and given to one of your stores?"

"This is not your concern anymore but as these are, what do you call them? *Verderblich*? *Verderblich*? Yes, as they are perishable, they will be shared between my comrades and me. You may go."

Rick stepped out into the fresh air and gave a low whistle, only to see Louis standing a few yards from him with folded arms and an unhappy expression that did not lighten as the American approached him. They walked slowly to the coach, and Rick told him what had happened.

"It's a little trick of theirs. Bananas can't be bought in the GDR normally, and because you were sarcastic to her, she got both her revenge and her treat as well. Look, Mr McCoy, you have caused problems on this trip, and we are only on the second day. I have the right to have you expelled from the group on the grounds of disruption, and it would be easier to do it here before we get properly into the Eastern Bloc, so final warning now, understand?" The American stopped Louis and said quietly: "You don't know how much I'm grateful to you for letting me stay on this trip. My thanks. I'll see you right one day."

Chapter Seven

As the coach travelled further east to the border and Poland, the travellers noticed how much the road traffic lessened compared with the hustle and bustle between Belgium and West Germany.

The condition of the autobahns was also worsening and no matter how he tried and cursed, Arnaud had to go over the majority of the potholes, although how the Trabant drivers managed to get from points 'a' to 'b' with their suspension was a source of wonder for him. "They must have balls made from concrete," he joked with the passengers behind him.

Louis reached for the microphone, and it was noticeable that even testing it to see it was on, had an effeminate sound. "*Phooh*...Ladies and gentlemen...*Phooh*...We will soon be coming to the border between the GDR and Poland. You might be interested to know that there is another Frankfurt, which is on the River Oder ahead, but we will pass by it until we get to a border crossing where on the Polish side is a small place called Zwiecko. The only important thing about Zwiecko I found out is that there was a concentration camp here during the last war. As we are already in communist Germany, we shouldn't be detained for too long, but I have to collect all your passports and then a Polish official will come to the coach and make sure the numbers tally. Now, I hope you know that Poland has been in a difficult time and there is a shortage—"

"So, no wisecracks about them. Got it, Rick, or do you want to see if the camp is still open?" shouted Arnaud.

"Roger and out!" exclaimed Rick, looking around the coach. "A guy could go nuts or bananas with that kind of wisecrack, folks."

"And as I said the other day, martial law ended in Poland so you won't see loads of troops," explained Louis. "It's up to you if you want to ask people in any chats you have with them, but I found they tend to go a bit quiet about what's been happening in the last few years. Here we are at the crossing."

They watched as Louis got off the coach and walked with their passports to the GDR guard who was standing with his Polish counterpart, and he handed them over to him. John and Tom looked at one another and back at the Polish official and had another stare.

"It can't be," said John.

"He's the spitting image," agreed Tom, shaking his head and causing Rick to listen in.

"Now hold on, guys, I'm the one who spots any Woodys on this trip," declared Rick, lifting himself up and looking in the direction where he saw Louis handing over the passports to the Polish border official. "What's so special about this little squirt? Er, sorry Tom, I meant the Polak."

"He's a pint-sized version of the Polish man in charge, General Jaruzelski[24], that's what," explained John, watching Louis and the official disappear into a small building to go through the passports. "The fellow who declared martial law."

"He's suffered some demotion?" observed Rick, without a trace of irony. "In charge of a country one moment and at a frontier fence the next. That's near what happened to General MacArthur[25] in Korea, boys; I should know."

After about five minutes, Louis reappeared with the Polish border guard in tow, and they came into the coach, the latter beginning his count. There was no doubt that apart from being two or three inches shorter than the Polish leader, the man bore an incredible likeness. There was the same pale, roundish face, hardly a chin to notice and a small, pointed nose and slightly slanting eyes that were behind tinted glasses. He also had a large forehead and despite a cap, signs of receding hair.

As he came to the centre of the coach where Tom, John and Rick were sitting, his counting was audible.

"...*Twenty-one, twenty-two…*"

"Sure hope you don't get bitter being reduced in the ranks, General, sir," said Rick.

"...*Blast, where was I?*"

The official returned to the front and began recounting until he came again to the three.

"Remember, the cream always rises back to the top," reminded Rick with an encouraging thumbs up.

The official stopped his counting and looked at the American, open-mouthed.

"What is this with the cream? I can't remember when I last had it. Now, was it twenty-two or thirty-two? Damn!"

Louis rushed down to where the Pole was standing with a pencil and scratching his head and, as the courier had dealt with him on previous trips, apologised in German, pointing at Rick.

"My apologies for this. We have a right pain in the arse with us on this trip."

The frontier guard considered Louis' words and shook his head, saluted to Rick and said to Louis: *"Ah, don't worry. I have the correct number back in the office. Who in their right mind wants to come to a country like this anyway when we can't get cream in the shops?"*

The group wandered around the impressive Old Market Square in the historic centre of Poznan but had arrived too late to see the mechanised billie goats butt one another at midday at the top of the clock tower in the Old Town Hall.

As they got to know one another more, John found himself in conversation with a Canadian woman who was travelling by herself. In her mid to late twenties, Martine came from Montreal, and with curly black hair and dark eyes, he found himself being attracted to her. The odd aspect to her was that despite her age, she had a brace on her top teeth.

"I hope you're enjoying the holiday so far?" he asked, politely.

"Oh, yes, it's so different from what I imagined. And your friend and the American have breathed some life into it."

"For better or for worse," he remarked. "I must say I admire you travelling by yourself."

"It's my way. I like Louis, don't you?" replied Martine, moving a little quicker ahead of him. "He seems cute. The driver's nice too, don't you think?"

He satisfied himself with a nod and watched as Martine gathered pace and caught up with Louis. You're on to a loser there, he thought to himself as he realised there was probably going to be little chance of a holiday romance blossoming with her.

As he looked to his right, he saw Rick and Tom walking along together, amused by the sight of these unlikely allies and wondering when would be the next time they could be butting horns like the goats on the clock tower. Rick looked back and caught sight of John, pointing to a bar and signalling that there was time for a drink before heading back to the coach for the next stage to Warsaw.

The three waited at the dingy bar counter for the barman to come to them, but he appeared more interested in talking to his regulars. It was only when Rick cleared his throat for the third time that the barman looked around and saw them, nodded and promptly went back to talking to his cronies. John and Tom saw that their companion was becoming riled by the episode and watched as he sidled up to the huddled group and slapped them on the shoulders, getting hold of one half empty glass and putting it near his lips.

"Yum! Yum!" he bellowed and pointed to the pumps, placing the glass heavily down on the counter and arching his eyebrows.

"Ronald Reagan…Maggie Thatcher…NATO…B52s!" he concluded putting his arms wide and making bombing sounds.

The Englishmen could not decide whether it was the names of the politicians they detested or the threat of a military strike, but the barman came quickly to the pump and poured insipid-looking lager for the three of them.

"Want Polish vodka?" he asked them, hoarsely. "Much better than Russian."

The three nodded in accord, and he reached for a bottle from one of the shelves behind the bar and gave it a kiss. "Best, better than my lover…much better than my wife, *krwawa krowa* (bloody cow)."

He watched them eagerly as they sipped at the vodka and smiled back in agreement. Looking at him with his bald head, sweaty lined face, missing teeth and a torn T-shirt, it was difficult for them to imagine him with a wife, let alone a lover. His fat, chubby and nicotine-stained fingers played a tune on the counter and then they came up and made a rotating movement.

"Wanna change money? I give good rate for dollar–zloty. You have West Mark, me too change."

Rick took a wallet from his jacket and flicked through the notes, producing a $10 note and placed it down on the counter. The bartender looked down and a sorry expression came upon him.

"Why not $100, mister?"

"Stay in Poland only two days, mister," replied Rick, smiling as he took another $10 note out. "That's my lot, now how many zlotys for me?"

The bartender considered the notes in front of them and looked at John and Tom but got shakes of the head. Next came a scratching of his forehead and a big sigh as he continued to deliberate.

"Okay, 200 zlotys."

The American chuckled and started putting the notes back in his wallet.

"Man, I've got here US dollars, not Eytie lira. Drink up, lads, and I'll give him a dollar for the drinks."

Rick's dismissive words caused an immediate hurt response from the bartender, and he grabbed hold of the American's hand with the dollar clenched in it and told him he had a better offer and took him down to the end of the counter where they successfully negotiated the deal. Both came back with a satisfied expression, and the Pole immediately replenished their beer and vodka.

"What's your name, friend?" asked Rick. "Not Lech as in Wałęsa, is it?"

The bartender shook his head vigorously and put a grimy finger to his lips.

"Bad name to say these days. Pity you not stay in Poznan longer. Have cousin. He a sailor in the Baltic merchant fleet. Has good deals when he comes back. Never mind, you know where Aleksander is here." He beamed, holding his arms wide and then hugging himself. "Call me Alek; I'm your friend when you come here again."

Alek looked at the two Englishmen and again at Rick who was disappearing into the gents.

"Your friend there, he very American, no?" he said to John. "Drive very hard deal with me."

"He's a second-hand car salesman," explained John. "We're English."

"Oh, never been. You have strong woman now, the chief," mumbled Alek with a pouting lower lip. "Ugly like my wife, bossy like my wife, maybe smells just like my wife. Many Poles here think Maggie a great person. She against Russians and communists. I say to them, 'Wanna be married to her?' They become communists again."

The Imperial Hotel reception in Warsaw was far from regal when they arrived and checked in with a receptionist who kept yawning, unintentionally showing how many fillings she had and declaring how tired she was.

As they were gathered waiting for the keys to go to their rooms, Louis introduced them to their local guide, Wiktor, for the following day. The man was in his thirties with sky blue eyes and an impressive beard that he stroked frequently and with a charming smile when introduced to any of the younger women, managing an *Enchanté* as he passed along them. The smile became fixed with the men, but it was the opportunity that John needed to see if he could track down and talk to Ewelina's family.

The guide was saying his farewells to the men and an *à bientôt* to the women when John managed to get his attention and introduce himself.

"Very pleased to meet you, John and welcome to Warsaw."

"I…want to ask a big favour and of course I…I understand if you feel it's not possible for you," stammered John, noticing the guide's eyes narrowing. "You see, some years ago I met a woman over here and she came to London, we got married but things—"

"Good time girl, John, after your nationality?" queried Wiktor, flatly.

"Well, probably but I wanted to explain to her family that I tried my best. She had a two-year-old child from a previous marriage, and if we had made the marriage last, we could have brought him over."

"Oh, big mess, John. Why meet? *Why*? Forget her and be happy. Find another one but a good woman next time."

"But if you could come along with me, if they don't speak English, I'd appreciate and…"

As he made the suggestion, John noticed Wiktor becoming more uneasy and the Pole started to look around him.

"Look, this is a private affair, and it is not, frankly, my problem, you understand?"

"I will pay you for your time and trouble—"

"It doesn't matter how many zlotys—"

"I'll make it dollars."

"Maybe we talk tomorrow during the tour. Goodnight."

John nodded and was about to find Tom when a hand came down on his shoulder and he turned to see Rick, staring down at him with a paternal smile.

"Forgive me for eavesdropping but that's a big, sad tale you had there. Tell me to mind my own business—"

"Mind your own business, Rick—"

"But that Polak had a point. I've been married three times, and I walked away from all of them without a backward glance, even one with two kids. And you're looking to make contact with a family of some tramp and a kid from another marriage? Come on, fellah, you must have taken legal advice?"

The legal advice centre was packed out that wintry, cold evening as John joined the queue and was asked to fill out a form as to why he was there for the free consultation.

He looked around him and realised that the majority would be there for housing issues, but with no money left after the period he had been with Ewelina when he had paid for everything, there was no other way he could get advice but *pro bono*. He completed the form and handed it to the receptionist who looked through it, her eyes showing little interest, and she nodded and placed it in a bundle at the top before taking it downstairs where the lawyers were.

After a while, three people were called, and as they disappeared, his lawyer appeared. He was a tall man in his forties with greying, sweptback hair and a nose that seemed as if it must be perpetually seeking out a higher vocation in life. His nostrils flared as he barked out: "Is Mr Murphy here?" On seeing John's hand raised, the nostrils flared even more, and the lawyer pointed to the stairs leading to the meeting room.

John's hopes of separate rooms where matters could be discussed confidentially were dashed. The small room had the lawyers and clients in the corners, and he went, without asking, to the unoccupied chairs, sitting down and hoping that their discussion would not be overheard as the other cases progressed. The lawyer stared at his form, sometimes muttering to himself and then looked up with a disbelieving snort.

"My name is Hubert Soames, Mr Murphy, and what a dreadful story yours is," he declared, staring wide-eyed at the form.

"I suppose you could say that," whispered John.

"Please speak up, I'm rather deaf, you know," confessed the lawyer.

His client wished silently the same condition could be afflicting the others in the room as he was asked to recite more details of what had happened to him. Before he had finished his story, John saw Soames scribble on his form and tut loudly, his eyes blazing and eyebrows dancing.

"Mr Murphy, do you mean to say this was a marriage of convenience?"

"It was bloody inconvenient for me," insisted John, trying to keep his voice down.

"That may be but tell me in all honesty, was the marriage *consummated*, Mr Murphy?"

"It depends what you mean by consummated," answered John, appalled by the direct question.

"By that I mean, was there penetration, never mind the ejaculation aspect until we need to come to that?"

"Er, that is…"

"…Oh, don't worry, Mr Murphy, no one here is concerned about this matter in the slightest!" bellowed the lawyer, leaning back with a sweep of his hand.

The lightest pin in the world could have been heard dropping in the room as Soames, eyes lit up with a thought, began snapping his fingers and leaning forward towards John. "I'll have a word with a colleague who is a bit more of an expert, Mr Murphy. Just you stay put while I do."

John cringed as he saw the two lawyers in deep conversation but with the other one talking into Soames' ear and the room full of his booming voice in response.

"Do you think so?…Yes, there was a leg over situation…One has been led to believe penetration occurred and…I see!"

Soames slapped his knees and stood, looking triumphantly at his abject client. "Good news, Mr Murphy, I do believe we can get her by her female short and curlies!"

John's memory of the legal advice centre made him shudder as Rick repeated his question, and while they made their way to the lift to take their luggage to the rooms, he explained the circumstances three years before. The American patted him on the shoulder, gave a long and low whistle and uttered: "You have all my sympathies, you poor, dumb jackass."

For most of the city tour, the group had gone by coach on the perimeter of the historic centre and saw the Palace of Culture that the majority felt was a concrete monstrosity dominating the city skyline with all the appearance of an unwelcome squatter.

While camera shutters could be heard elsewhere on their tour there was a silence as the coach came to a halt, and they were allowed out to view the building. Arnaud and Louis watched the group, amused by the way they looked nonplussed by it.

"Hey, Wiktor, what do you Poles call this?" asked Arnaud, winking and knowing the answer.

"There are quite a number of names…Do you want the polite ones or the most common?"

The group gathered around their local guide and one elderly Englishman with a walking stick and Panama hat cleared his throat and said: "Look here, some of us are still true to the cause, you know and want none of this disrespect, just the facts."

"I am sorry, sir, and I will not give you any disrespect, I promise," answered Wiktor. "This, ladies and gentlemen, is the Palace of Culture and Science, so named by the General Secretary of the Soviet Union as a gift that was opened in 1956. Originally, it was called the Joseph Stalin Palace of Culture and Science, but as he was found *not* to be true to the cause, after his death, his name was dropped. But we have a long memory in this country, and it is known fondly by us Poles as Stalin's Syringe due to its shape, although there are other less respectful descriptions of what it resembles. Now, I suggest that we hunt out some real culture on our trip."

Tom and John were by the old gentleman and heard him muttering: "Bloody Poles…no better than a bunch of fascists themselves before the war." He looked at them and nodded briskly. "Oh, yes, most of them were; only Czechoslovakia was a liberal democracy – bourgeois democracy as we say. And guess who backed Hitler and the Munich Agreement in '38 and snatched a bit of Czechoslovakia for themselves? The bloody Poles! The rest were all bloody fascists – Hungary, Romania and Bulgaria, or as close as damn it. And this young bugger goes and mocks what was done for them. My name's Harold Potter, by the way. Jolly nice to meet you."

Standing in front of the Chopin monument in Aazienki Park, Wiktor's chest visibly swelled with pride as he waited for the group to assemble before him, his eyes showing a fervour of what he was about to say.

"Ladies and gentlemen, you are standing, not only in the most beautiful park in Poland but in probably – no, certainly – the most beautiful park in the world…Aazienki Park!"

"No, it isn't," said Harold Potter, shaking his head determinedly.

"I tell you, sir…sir, I did not catch your name from our last stop. Your name?" enquired an increasingly irritated Wiktor. "You are an expert of public parks and gardens, I take it?"

"When you have been to the Jardin du Luxembourg in Paris, or the Villa Doria Pamphili in Rome, then you can tell me what is the most beautiful park in the world, young man," replied Harold, whose voice grew in confidence as he spoke. "And to show that I am not against the New World and its attempts, perhaps you could give me your view of the Golden Gate Park in San Francisco? My name is Doctor Harold Potter, botanist, retired, at Kew Gardens…so, no expert at all, what?" he added, looking around at the smiling audience, taking off his pebble glasses and giving them a wipe. "Oh, just to show you I'm not partisan; forgot to mention my own little place! Sorry, do carry on, young man."

This Wiktor did, plainly ruffled by the diminutive botanist who had dared to challenge his boast but who carried on, nonetheless, citing the attractions of the park. He then turned to the statue behind him and breathed in deeply, his hand stretched before the monument, and he turned back to the travellers, a triumphant smile on his face.

"And this, ladies and gentlemen, is a statue erected in 1926 to the immortal Frédéric Chopin, without doubt the greatest composer of all time!"

"And how do you substantiate that claim?" came the disbelieving voice of an elderly lady who might have been a twin of Harold Potter with her tiny appearance and pebble glasses but in a prim dress and floppy hat.

"Fucking hell, another lunatic," muttered Wiktor, under his breath. "Good lady, perhaps you could say why this genius does not rate highly enough with you?"

"Well, young man, for one, he wrote only two piano concertos while Mozart composed twenty-three."

"Well, dare I say, one cannot go by quantity alone, I think you will agree."

"And how many symphonies, operas or masses, or indeed concertos for other instruments did your Chopin manage, eh?"

"Ah, a very interesting point, good lady, and your name is?" asked an increasingly disconsolate local guide.

"Carmen Clay, retired piano teacher at the Royal College of Music."

The Pole's eyes went skyward and then returned quickly to her, followed by a forced, if not pained smile.

"Oh, your name is Clay and the gentleman's is Potter. What an amazing coincidence," he exclaimed, applauding them but whispering in Polish: *"Both as cracked as one another.* Are there any other questions?"

Wiktor saw a hand go up from the crowd and a loud American accent say: "What's it with the lack of harmony from this fellah Lech Wałęsa and the Solidarity mob?"

"I can assure you, sir, that there is nothing to say about either, and they will not feature on the rest of my tour with you, of that you can be assured because they are of no consequence to Poland as it is now."

Wiktor waited for the tourists to gather around him, and once more, his chest expanded with pride as he talked about the magnificent reconstruction of the Old Town around them.

"Now, ladies and gentlemen, I will not say that it is the best Old Town in the world because I am a modest man, especially since I met Mr Potter and Miss Clay. But I would like you to look around you and you will think you are back in the medieval and baroque periods. You would be right, but you would also be wrong. Why this contradiction? Today is 31 August and you know what that means? It means tomorrow, the 1 September, was the outbreak of the attack by Nazi Germany on Poland and so the start of the Second World War when on 3 September, Britain and France declared war on Hitler. We lost our part of the war and so began a very brutal period for the Polish people, as you know. What the Nazis did when they retreated from the Red Army in 1944 was the destruction of a whole city. They blew up over 90% of it, including the Old Town. So, what you see here, ladies and gentlemen is the recreation out of the ruins of what had been. It is most remarkable, is it not? Think of the time, effort and resources to rebuild these places and make them look as they were and at a time when Poland was recovering from the devastation of what Goebbels said was total war. Four years ago, UNESCO recognised this by declaring the Old Town a World Heritage Site and…and…"

Wiktor's moving description was being drowned out from a side street and the group moved to see what was happening and despite him urging them to remain by his side, he had to follow the travellers to where a demonstration appeared to be taking place. A large gathering had unfurled flags with just one word *Solidarność* in heavy red lettering. The crowd were holding up their hands in a 'V' for victory salute and after a couple of speeches, began singing the national anthem with mounting fervour:

"Jeszcze Polska nie umarła,	"Poland has not yet died,
Kiedy my żyjemy	So long as we still live.
Co nam obca moc wydarła	What the alien power has seized from us,
Szablą odbijemy…"	We shall recapture with a sabre…"

"What did the speakers say?" asked one of the older Australian women. "I thought you said that Solidarity was nothing now?"

"Look, they are nothing," answered a very annoyed Wiktor. "They are just agitators. Solidarity means nothing to most Polish people now. They were good at the beginning but got too big for their boots. Don't you understand? We could have been invaded by the Russians if they had carried on in the way they did."

"But it was wrong to suppress them, surely?" said the other Australian woman.

"I am your local guide, not a political commentator," he snapped back. "Look, if the regime is that bad, why did they release 35,000 political prisoners last month when they celebrated the fortieth anniversary of the People's Republic? We have difficult times but give us the chance and we will get back to normality for us. Please, we must leave and go back to the coach before anything happens between the police, if they arrive, and the agitators."

The coach party were jabbering all the way back to the hotel, talking about what they had seen and observing how sharp Wiktor had become when being put under pressure on what turned out to be the vexed question of Solidarity.

He sat sullenly next to Louis, not saying a word until they got to the Imperial and as John waited behind him and Wiktor, heard the local guide say: "We Poles are a proud people, and we don't like being talked down to, especially by two geriatrics and ignorant Australian women. I hope the next group you bring through aren't so bad as this lot. It's all right for them; they'll get back to fully stocked shops and no informers about and…"

The words trailed off as he watched the party disappear into the reception and turned and spotted John waiting. But the Pole was in a furious mood and the blue eyes flashed angrily at him, his face flushed by the afternoon's events.

"You still want to go on this pointless exercise, I suppose?" he said.

"I understand this hasn't been an ideal day for you, but I thought we had an agreement, and I'm willing to reward your time and help," reminded John, taking the wallet from his jacket and flicking through the notes and offering them to the guide. "Will $20 be enough?"

Wiktor held up his hand and came close to John.

"Are you bloody mad? Handing me western currency outside a hotel and anybody could be watching!" Wiktor hissed. "Go on, make me out to be a speculator, will you? Just give me the note with the address and phone number, and we'll see if it's possible in the first place. Who will be there as far as you know?"

"Only the father and brother. The mother died a few years ago."

John apologised and watched the guide go to a public phone booth in front of the hotel while he followed and came up close and watched the Pole dial and wait for an answer. After a while, he saw Wiktor look at him and give a thumbs up and speak loudly into the phone: *"Hello, hello. Is that Mr Gniewek, father of Ewelina? An Englishman who says he was married to your daughter has arrived in Warsaw and has asked me if it is possible to come and see you…?…Is he that arsehole? He seems a decent man to me. It's up to you. He just wants me to translate and I think, explain…Yes, I have your address. We'll be along within 20 minutes. Just remember, he may be a bit naive but a genuine man."*

Wiktor put the receiver back and blew out his cheeks before coming back to John and gave him a long look.

"John, you are absolutely sure you wish to go through with this? For the moment, don't worry about the money."

"I have to try and explain. I wanted to be a proper husband and…"

"…Then, the father said you sounded like an…a…good man and he welcomes us. We'll get the tram there; it runs well at this time of the day."

Wiktor began to run when he saw sight of a red and yellow Konstal tram that made slow progress to the stop. He noticed John's problem keeping up with him and pointed at him to the driver. They got on at the rear with the guide paying for the two of them.

"My apologies, John, I didn't notice you have a bad leg," said Wiktor. "I try and learn colloquial English and you have a term called 'gammy', I believe?"

"It'll do as an alternative," agreed John.

As they sat down on the hard seats, John looked around him at the half-filled carriage and saw a couple who were already drawing attention from the other passengers. In their early thirties, the man sat saying nothing but with a gormless, drunken smile on his face, listened with a bored expression to his wife starting to berate him, at first quietly but then increasing the volume because he just grinned back at her. Their clothes were frayed and despite their apparent age, it looked like life was already a big struggle, especially when John saw tears trickling down the woman's cheeks.

"You rotten, drunk bastard. What are you?"

Silence.

"Your parents are throwing us out of the flat because you roll up drunk every night. Happy with that, shitbag?"

More silence and a smile.

The woman stood up and gave him a slap around the face.

The man looked around at the other passengers and grinned.

The woman slapped him twice around the face, and he smiled back at her.

"Would you smile if I chewed your balls off and spat them out?"

He nodded, causing the carriage passengers to stifle their laughter as she flew into a rage at them.

"Go on, you fuckers, laugh away but try dealing with this every day of the week. God above, help me!"

While the other passengers looked away at her words, John maintained a sympathetic stare at her, which it was clear she misread.

"And what the hell do you think you're looking at, you bastard?"

Wiktor stood and leaned towards the woman and stated clearly: *"Madam, this man is an English academic and is studying the romantic behaviour of Polish couples towards one another."*

"I see, then let me help your research with a final demonstration, Professor!" she yelled, clenching her fist and hitting her husband on the jaw, knocking him sideways and unconscious. She surveyed the carriage passengers around her and thumped her chest, declaring with a triumphant smile, *"Float like a butterfly, sting like a Queen bee!"*

The tram dropped the two off in Abrahama Street, near some daunting tower blocks, and they made their way to one of them.

The sign stated that the lift was out of order, and they climbed the stairs, which smelled of urine until they got to the eighth floor, walking to a battered brown door. Wiktor knocked on it as the bell made no sound. He knocked again and began whistling a song until he heard the sound of someone coming to the door and opening it slowly. A thin-faced man in his mid-fifties looked at them with grey, dull eyes and nodded, waving them through and shutting the door behind.

A small front room was cluttered with chairs and a big table. The ashtray on it was full to overflowing with cigarette stubs and the air was heavy with their smell. Looking around to a mantelpiece, John could see the biggest framed photograph was of a woman the same age as the man. Hanging from the wall was a large image of Pope John Paul II giving the sign of the cross and smiling. John's eyes came back to the mantelpiece where there was an old black and white photo of the man and woman with two children. The boy was tall and leaning against his father while the one of the girl already had that mocking smile he knew so well.

"Hello, there of me and family," said Mr Gniewek gruffly in halting English. He looked to Wiktor and shrugged. "No really English. Son he has. Come a while. Sit. *Wódka? Spiritus?*"

Wiktor chuckled and looked at John, saying: "He wants to kill you for marrying his daughter."

"I had *Spiritus* in 1980 when I came to Poland," replied John, smiling at the memory.

"Okay, what did you dilute it with?" enquired Wiktor.

"I didn't. I had it neat."

"That's impossible, it's 95% volume!" exclaimed Wiktor, eyes open.

"You've got to understand I had the Irish equivalent many times – *potcheen* – so it was like a small step up to *Spiritus*. Or if I had had any more, the spirit world."

Wiktor quickly explained to Gniewek and he in turn, looked with admiration at the Englishman and shook his hand, declaring: *"This man is no arsehole, after all!"*

"Mr Gniewek said…he said…he praises your liver and you," declared Wiktor. "But I think we had better stick to vodka to make sure we remember what is said this evening. *Vodka, yes, please, Mr Gniewek."*

As he was pouring the vodka, the door was heard opening and shutting, and in a moment, a tall man in his thirties was in the room looking down at them seated at the table. There was a similarity in features with his sister although he was slimmer in build and from his initial demeanour appeared to be straightforward in character.

"Good evening to you both. Which one is John?" The Englishman rose and shook hands while Wiktor introduced himself. "I hope you don't mind if I don't drink vodka? I try to keep my head clear during the daytime. If my father didn't mention, my name is Marek. Now, I'll have some juice instead. We'll carry on in English, and I'll explain to my father later."

When he returned, he stood by the mantelpiece as John told them what had occurred between him and Ewelina as they listened without interruption. "I'm so sorry and when I decided to come on this trip via Warsaw, it was a perfect opportunity to meet you both to let you know I meant the best to happen but only the worst did."

"We felt very unhappy when she left for London, John, because we knew she was probably doing this without much thought for what she was leaving behind," stated Marek. "I mean her son who you didn't know existed."

"Where is he now?" asked John.

"First he stayed with the former in-laws because she said she would return in a month, but when it was clear she was going to stay, the father took him and that's where he is now. He's remarried, and they are happy. We often see them. It's good, very good. But what can I say of Ewelina? She has a sense of unreality of her situation. What is the word, John, of someone who loves themselves more than others?

"Vanity; they are vain."

"Yes, yes, she was, and I suppose she still is, in London. Every man must love or admire her and if he doesn't or stops, the fault is with him, not her." Marek watched John give a slight nod. "Her first husband walked out because he found out what was going on behind his back and you did the same, but I believe after a couple of months? That was the first sensible thing you did after meeting her. But truth to tell, you had no need to come here to tell us about Ewelina; we knew it, but she carried on even when Mother was dying."

"I thought it was maybe the death that made her unstable because she seemed so different from meeting her here in Warsaw and when she came," remarked John.

"No, if she said that it was really because she couldn't get herself a ready babysitter for when she went clubbing and other, shall we say, entertainments."

"We had a Polish landlady for a while, and when we broke up, she said: 'I'm sorry, Mr Murphy, but Ewelina isn't a responsible person.' She understood."

"Excuse me for butting in on this, this family matter," apologised Wiktor, "but John, you must understand what it is like these days when Polish people have the chance to get to the West. They see it as the great promised land and they'll do anything, even by deceit to get there. That's even if they see it isn't…Oh, you have that famous saying, where the pavements aren't paved with gold. Our history has made some of us desperate, and we grasp at what or who we can, sometimes with very cruel results."

"Then I will add to the cruelty," said Marek, finishing off the glass in his hand. "This meeting is not for our benefit but for you and yours alone, John. You want us to sympathise with you, to slap you on the back because you want to be seen as the innocent person. You were a fool to marry her. You aren't a young man with stars in his eyes. Ewelina is what she is and I am certain you have friends and relatives who questioned what you did getting involved with her. If I have anyone to blame for this mess, it's you. You'll go on with your holiday and go back to London thinking it's a job well done. It's not. It's John with his conscience that will be happy. What's for us? We struggle with this bastard life, queuing for things you can get just like that. I mean even toilet paper to wipe our arses, John. People fighting one another like snakes in the pit. We're ordinary people, John. We can't get dollars and head to the Pewex[26] shops without queues unless we become Party-loving jerks or criminals. Think of that when you next have a shit."

All that could be heard in the room for the next minute was the sound of a clock on the mantelpiece as John took in the sudden turn in the conversation. He thought of denying Marek's blunt words but could only look glumly at the empty glass in his hand. When he glanced up at Marek's father, he saw the older man staring at him and sucking on his cigarette before looking at his watch. It was the signal to leave and John stood with Wiktor.

"Thank you for meeting us," whispered John, but there was no reply. Marek raised his hand and walked into the kitchen, and the father showed them the way to the front door, closing it as they stood by the stairs without a farewell.

As they walked away silently from the tower block, Wiktor suggested they take a taxi back to the hotel to save time, and he realised the Englishman needed to absorb Marek's damning assessment.

"Don't get too sensitive of Marek; he's a bitter man, made so by his selfish sister," advised Wiktor clambering into the cab. "I'd probably be the same."

"But if I hadn't had met her—"

"She'd have got her claws into some other Westerner. This sounds bad, but you were a soft touch for her. I'm one to try and remember your expressions, so here goes. When you met her, she was like butter wouldn't melt in her mouth, yes? But when she knew she had got you involved, the butter went rancid, yes?"

Wiktor's use of the expression managed to bring a smile to John's lips.

"So, now you know what was probably in your mind anyway. Forgive me but the woman you fell for was from a pigsty but don't get too cynical. She sounds a crazy person who will carry on hurting other people till someone will hurt her more. At least this trip has shown you a bit more about the Polish character you don't get in your Western reports."

"You know that it's a bit ironic that the media are very pro-Solidarity as a union but very anti them when it comes to my own country," noted John. "And Thatcher is the same."

"She walks on water here, John."

"I'd like to test that in mid-Atlantic," answered the Englishman with a bitter tone.

"She comes second to the Pope, who I'm sure will one day be made a saint for defeating…" Wiktor stopped as he realised the cab driver had not said a word and appeared to be listening to the conversation. "It's a slight irony that the Pope, who has been critical of actions here, can be repressive and sack liberal theologians and be damning of the Church of Liberation in Latin America. Maybe it's a trait we have in Poland of not listening to the other side. What do *you* think?" The observation was said in English by Wiktor directly to the driver's mirror.

"As long as you pay the fare, don't worry. I don't give a damn about politics or religion, mate."

Wiktor smiled at the retort and supposed the cab driver had understood enough but was unlikely to be a snake in the grass.

"My favourite person is the cab driver, John, because he will get you from Point A to Point B with a little deviation via Point C if you don't know the route. But he'll get you there. That's more than our leaders can do…they keep stalling the cab. Yes, he may be cynical…"

"…We're *bloody* cynical!" chirped in the cab driver in English.

"Thank you, driver. Now, here's back to reality, I wonder if we can keep to our agreement, John?" asked Wiktor with a nod and cupped hand. "Maybe a little more to get me home and brush up on my English too?"

John walked to the reception desk and waited for the same blonde receptionist to come when she had finished talking on the phone.

The night was still young, but he wondered if Tom had decided to make a sensible decision of early to bed than hit the town after his experience in Berlin. The receptionist finished her call and came to the desk, yawning again and displaying her full dental record for him.

"Yes? I am tired," she stated to confirm any suspicions.

"Is my friend Mr Laurel in his room or gone out?" he enquired, giving the room number. After a cross face by the receptionist at having to walk to check on the pigeonhole, she came back with a folded message that read: 'Gone with

69

Rick to the nightclub at the top floor of the hotel with the others. Should be fun. Tom.'

The words 'fun' and 'Tom' did not sit together naturally and John contemplated whether to play safe or find what escapades were yet to come, starting with the delights of the nightclub.

"What's the nightclub's name?" he asked, watching another comprehensive display of fillings flash in front of his eyes.

"Pussies Galore."

John's contemplation deepened.

The massive bouncer asked for John's hotel card, examined and let him through to a cavernous, darkened room with music immediately assaulting his ears.

He squinted to get used to the poorly lit surroundings but also the pall of cigarette smoke that billowed around the ceiling and drifted downwards. But the noise of *Somebody's Watching Over Me* hit him as his eyes gradually became accustomed, and in the distance, he could see some of the coach party grouped together, including Tom and Rick. There was also Martine who was trying to persuade Louis to join her on the dance floor and Pip who was there already in a lively threesome with the Australian girls. They were unaware of Tom's baleful gaze as he talked with Rick and by the nearby bar, stood Arnaud, still with his tinted glasses and chatting to a barmaid.

"So, you're back," remarked Tom when John joined them. "Did you get what you wanted?"

"More of a flea in my ear than a warm greeting," replied John, looking around at the near-empty nightclub. "You and Rick were right; it was best to let sleeping dogs lie."

"And talking about dogs, guess who's been chatting to us?" hinted Rick with a tilted head to nearby chairs where two women were waiting to be joined. "Tom here has danced with one of them already when they did the smoochy music, and they say more's coming up. Are you game for the tall one, buddy? Our kind of music is just starting."

Tom licked his lips and nodded, approaching the taller of the two and bent down to whisper in her ear.

"Oh, how much has he had to have?" asked John.

"Not enough to notice her Adam's apple, pal."

John's eyes widened at the revelation, and he looked at Rick and then at Tom who appeared to be having some difficulty persuading the woman to be a dance partner. John had to admit there was a rather masculine aspect to the object of Tom's desire with her strapless dress showing unusually muscular shoulders and arms. Her hair was perhaps a little too tidy, and when she eventually nodded to dance, it appeared to move *en masse* before being corrected. As Tom passed John, arm in arm, he looked at his friend with an air of triumph.

"Wanda has agreed to dance till she drops," he informed John, smirking.

"Why not?" came the rather deep response from Wanda.

"Drops what? Before you do, Tom, can I have a word?" John muttered into Tom's ear.

"No, you'll have to find your own partner, so try Wanda's friend."

With that, Tom tried to take Wanda in his arms to the sound of Tina Turner's *What's Love Got to do with it*, but it was soon evident who was taking the lead. John looked to his right and another hopeless sight greeted him as Martine was visibly getting frustrated by Louis's indifferent dancing and minimal conversation. As the dance came to the end, she nodded briefly to him and walked determinedly to the bar where Arnaud waited with a smile on his face and immediately commenced a conversation she welcomed.

John looked around him and saw that Rick had gone and started chatting with a young woman sitting alone by the bar, and he decided to go and plonk himself on the remaining seat by Wanda's friend. She moved her chair closer to his and attempted a sweet smile. With short dark hair and slight body, she was not quite in the Hotel Bristol class and was dressed as if she had just come from an office job.

"H-e-l-l-o," she said slowly.

"H-e-l-l-o," he replied.

"Are you staying at the hotel?"

"I am. Why?"

"What is your name?"

"John, what's yours?"

"My name's Ewelina…"

John's eyes bulged and swivelled as he turned to take a closer look and check but no, the face and voice were quite different.

"Er, why do you want to know about if I'm staying here?"

Her hand came down quickly and decisively on his knee and squeezed it provocatively.

"Because for $40 we can have fantastic sex together!" promised Ewelina, sipping her drink with her tongue playing along the glass. "Sex you will never forget…and neither will I."

"Oh, I'm sorry, but I've just started the holiday and have to be careful with my money," explained John.

"Mmm, what about $20?"

"You see, I have a budget and—"

"What about a dance for a dollar?" she asked with an air of resignation, and when John again apologised for his decision, she nodded, eased herself out of the chair and walked away.

John considered that a chaste evening might be dull but would leave him feeling more rested in body and mind than whatever Ewelina 2 had in mind. He looked to the bar, and there was Arnaud's arm around Martine's compliant waist, Rick was patting a young woman's hand who had become his companion. His hand was waving in front of her, and he pointed with his finger in a downward direction. Further along, Pip had his arms on both Joan and Jean's shoulders. All that was needed to complete the romantic liaisons was to see Tom oblivious to Wanda's real nature. John searched for the couple on the dance floor and his eyes alighted on the bizarre sight of them in a close clinch, swaying rhythmically to Englebert Humperdinck's *The Last Waltz*. Suddenly, Tom leapt backwards, staring wildly at Wanda and sped away, coming to John, open-mouthed.

"Any problem?" enquired John, innocently.

"She had a bump where no bump should be!"

"Hernia?" suggested John.

"Sometimes, Murphy, you *really* annoy me!"

Chapter Eight

The wait just over the Soviet Union side of the border near Brest was difficult for the coach party to comprehend.

The traffic was virtually non-existent now and given it was going to be a long journey before their first overnight stop in Minsk, impatience was beginning to mount among many of them, along with the uncomfortable, sultry weather. Others, like Pip and his young friends, seemed not to care as their inane conversation had moved on from Bali to Tahiti and was doing more to irritate Tom than anything else. Of course, there was also the second night where he had found himself in an embarrassing situation never experienced at home in London. The wait and the memories made him seek comfort in Arnaud's Belgian beer.

"I hope what occurred last night won't be repeated to anyone, John?" he requested, despondently looking ahead and then glugging down the beer.

"You mean…?"

"…Of my mistaking that person as…"

"…Did you get to grips with Wanda's wand, buddy?" enquired Rick, dispelling any hopes of secrecy that Tom might have hoped for. "Gee, a sumo wrestler on the dance floor in sequins would have looked more feminine than your gal, Tom."

"Rick, please keep a confidence for once in your life," said Tom through gritted teeth.

"My word as a gentleman," assured Rick, slapping his thigh and nodding at the discomfited Englishman.

But once having finished the sentence, he went down to the front of the coach and had a few words with Louis, who nodded in return. The American took the microphone and turned to the fellow coach travellers and declared: "Well, we seem to be here for a while, guys and gals, so how about me doing a little number? No, not Sinatra but this is one for my great l'il pal, Wood…er…Tom

73

here after his fantastic success with the opposite sex last night. You must have heard this at breakfast?"

"Yes, we did!" shouted back the travellers, almost in one amused voice to Tom's mortification.

"Then, here's a number that'll get Tom rocking with your kinky Kinks[27]," promised Rick.

Well, I'm not the world's most passionate guy,
But when I looked in her eyes,
Well, I almost fell for my Wanda,
Wa Wa Wa Wa Wanda.
Girls will be boys, and boys will be girls.
It's a mixed up, muddled up, shook up world,
Except for Wanda. Wa Wa Wa Wa Wanda.
Well, I left home just a week before,
And I've never ever kissed a woman before,
But Wanda smiled and took me by the hand,
And said: "Little boy, gonna make you a man."
Well, I'm not the world's most masculine man,
But I know what I am, and I'm glad I'm a man,
And so is Wanda.
Wa Wa Wa Wa Wanda…
"Wa…*Why*, hello there!"

Rick broke off his singing as he spotted at the entrance to the coach a smiling woman who came up the steps and nodded to Louis and Arnaud. She was a strikingly tall brunette in her thirties with classic Slavonic features of high cheekbones and an attractive upturned nose. Her full lips were accentuated by a generous application of bright red lipstick. What brought her even more to life were dazzling blue eyes and a mischievous smile, displaying perfect white teeth. Despite the close day, her dress was modest with a white lavender blouse done up almost to the neck and a pleated skirt that covered most of her legs.

"I am sorry to stop your aria, sir. Good day to you and" – she gazed down to the rest of the party – "and to all of you, dear travellers. Welcome to the Soviet Union. My name is Dina."

"And welcome to Rick, dear Dina. May I say as a world-weary man from Uncle Sam—"

The Intourist guide looked at the American with amusement. "That of all the coaches in all the world I had to walk into your one?"

The expression baffled Rick but not some of the travellers who chuckled at the *Casablanca*[28] allusion. He returned to his seat and scowled at Tom and John. "Watch this one, she might know too much. Remember, from this point, we're in KGB country."

Dina greeted Arnaud and Louis with smiles and handshakes and took the microphone and started: "Please forgive the delay. I was on a late train from Moscow, and the travel to you was a little chaotic. But again, you are most welcome to my land, and I hope that over the next eight days or so you will find much to entertain you and I hope, impress you too. You know that the Soviet Union is made up of many nationalities, and we are now in one of the republics – Belorussia[29]. Its capital is Minsk, and as it is some hours away, why not relax as we drive along, and I will tell you more about it and other facts that will interest you. But one that I must inform you immediately is that our comfort breaks for toilet will not be in the usual facilities because I must be frank, they are not best for you. So, I strongly suggest when there is a need, we will go into a wooded area and relieve ourselves there. Believe me, you will be grateful for this choice."

"We go in separate groups, Rick, just to let you know!" shouted Arnaud.

"Jeez, haven't you ever heard of consenting adults, pal?" complained Rick. "Hey, fellas, there was plenty of consensual activity next room where he was with the Canadian broad," he whispered to Tom and John. "It went on so long and loud I was going to bang on the wall and ask for a threesome." Rick leant across and gave Tom a friendly poke. "Sorry, that must seem a tad rude for a servant of the British Crown?"

"You would be surprised at the shared experience," muttered Tom. "Although my offer was received, not sent."

"Well?"

"Well, what?"

"Did you take the offer up?"

"I have no intention of replying to coarse questions," declared Tom, opening his book of George Orwell's *1984* and looking at the print.

"Okay, that's a 'No' then?"

Tom slammed the book shut and gave Rick a withering look.

"What does it take for you to stop your bloody blathering?"

"I was going to ask for tongues but a peck on the cheek will do," replied Rick, pretending to look hurt.

As he finished his sentence, Tom leaned across and much to the surprise of all those nearby, pecked Rick firmly on the cheek.

"Now, belt up!"

Reasonable progress was made by the coach along the near-deserted motorway until after a few whispers by the women passengers, Arnaud pulled over in a suitable spot.

While the men relieved themselves against the trees, they could only imagine how it must be for some of the women on the trip. The concern was particularly voiced by Harold Potter who gave bashful glances in the direction of the ladies partially hidden in the long grass and trees.

"I do think this is most inelegant for them," he commented. "One's heart must go out to the likes of Carm…er, Miss Clay."

Rick hoisted his member from his trousers and looked down on the botanist without sympathy.

"How'd you reckon the squaws on the plains did it? In a perfumed water closet?"

"Why, no, Mr McCoy, but they were used to performing nature's act in this manner," explained Potter politely to Rick. "And I believe Miss Clay was rather too delicate for the Girl Guides where such performances may have been expected."

Rick completed his sprinkle and quickly returned his manhood to his pants and zipped up his trousers, still observing the companion with some disbelief.

"How ever did you manage to gain an empire? I guess I know how you came to lose it," he stated to Potter.

"Some imperialist reactionaries believed it was by giving women the vote in 1918," remarked Potter with an embarrassed smile.

"Sure it wasn't failing to make membership of the Girl Guides compulsory?" queried the American.

"What a novel thought!" noted a smiling Potter, scratching the side of his head. "We really must find the answer by the next comfort break."

With one further comfort stop on the way and no answer to Rick's probing question, the coach arrived in Minsk in the early evening.

The first meal in the Soviet Union proved to set the standard of what was to follow.

After a watery soup with a few lank vegetables and stale rye bread, the main course comprised a tough steak from an unknown animal and tinned carrots and peas. Plain ice cream and rock-hard biscuits completed the feast. But on the bright side, the drinkers noticed the waiters had opened large bottles of good beer from Leningrad and placed them on all the tables. There followed the first of many occasions where the temperate were pestered by the thirsty for their alcohol going begging.

An evening stroll in the centre of Minsk proved to be disappointing because they witnessed wide, soulless boulevards with daunting concrete buildings and little where the citizens could relax in the form of cafés, bars and restaurants.

But as Dina had poignantly explained on the way, some 80% of Minsk was destroyed by the Nazis after the invasion of 1941 on a scale similar to Warsaw. The priority here had been to build for work and accommodation, not leisure and no one could doubt it had been achieved here but in a brutal style.

While John tried to vainly persuade Tom to come and investigate what appeared to be a bar with flashing blue lights, he noticed Rick near to it with a woman. But instead of entering it, the couple passed by and were engaged in a lively conversation with the occasional nod from the American. From what he could see, the woman was middle-aged and an unlikely partner in Rick's kind of erotic pursuit. Yet with his undoubted libido undiminished with age, John logged it down to another carnal conquest by the Yank.

"Good evening, do you want to change money?"

The enquiry made the pair turn and see a short, stout man looking at them with a smile. He was as far away from a black marketer as could be imagined, looking smart in a light grey suit and tie and his forehead wrinkled in anticipation.

"The official rate is one rouble to the pound sterling," he said flatly. "I can give you two roubles."

It was nowhere as generous as what John bought in zlotys in Warsaw and he felt reluctant to get involved with a deal in the open. Tom had already decided to walk in the direction of the hotel, telling him he would be at the bar and leaving his friend to disappoint the man.

"I'm sorry, but no."

"Okay, hope you enjoy your stay here, but you won't get a better rate from anyone else," advised the man, turning on his heel and quickly moving away into the night.

John watched him and waited to see if he had been joined by anyone else, or that there might be police in the shadows, but no one was visible. It was relatively early in the evening, but it was striking how empty this part of Minsk was for a capital city.

John looked around the hotel hard currency bar and was struck by how different it was from the rouble alternative on the other side.

In here were plush chairs and the décor was in delicate blues and pinks with a floor that was made from parquet timber of what appeared the highest quality. A narrow entrance to one side had the words in Cyrillic and Latin texts, which both ornately explained a casino awaited. A big and bored bouncer in an impressive dinner jacket was propped up by a counter next to the door.

John could just about make out dark figures inside the casino, and as his eyes searched for Tom, there were a few pretty blonde women talking, laughing to one another at the bar and all smoking heavily while waiting for the evening's business to commence. No matter what economic system was in place, the oldest profession remained open for discussion and negotiation. Minsk proved no different from Warsaw in that respect, and from what he could observe, he felt confident in telling Tom there was no equivalent to Wanda to challenge him. An attractive barmaid was ready to take an order from him, and he was tempted to reach for his wallet when:

"Do we have to drink here?"

John turned around and there was Tom, making a mental note of the ladies and possible dangers ahead.

"In my opinion, the rouble bar will be cheaper and safer than here. If you wish to stay, that's up to you."

For once, John couldn't disagree with his friend. Prices would be higher, even in this backwater of the Soviet Union and the exchange at the hotel reception would tide them over in the rouble bar.

The contrast with the hard currency bar was stark. They walked into a quiet, subdued space with furniture that had drab, peeling wallpaper and a framed photograph of Leonid Brezhnev[30], the recently dead leader of the Soviet Union, seemed to confirm that this would not be the liveliest of haunts in Minsk. In truth, the barman looked as if he could prove the deceased was in a livelier condition as he held his head in his hands and elbows propped up on the counter. A few customers were present, sipping at their drinks, and from their silence, they were there more to contemplate their lonely lives than have a good time.

As they came to the bar and wake the dead behind it, a hesitant voice was heard to their rear: "Hello, do you speak English?"

When they turned, they saw a young man in his twenties, and by the dark but pitted olive skin and deep brown eyes, along with jet-black hair and accent, they could tell his home was far from the Soviet Union.

"We are English," replied John, noting that the man was tentative in their presence. "And you?"

"From Columbia, sir, a student at the university here in Minsk. I study engineering. My name is Jesus. No, really, I haven't chosen my second coming in Minsk. There are better places," he whispered.

A joke like that relaxed them, and they invited him to join them for a drink and ordered from the bar, sitting near it and spurring the comatose barman into life. The barman came with the drinks, and they noticed how Jesus gripped the glass delicately, moving it around before he lifted it to his lips and sipped slowly, closing his eyes.

"Thank you, my friends, they serve good beer here, and I have little opportunity to come and meet people like you. You are on holiday here?"

Tom explained the details while John remained silent, watching the nervousness of the man as he bit frequently at his fingernails, nodding quickly and blinking often. His wish to know what was happening outside the Soviet Union was clear and that included in the UK.

"I hear there is much trouble in your country. The miners and demonstrations against all the weapons the Americans are sending. All the unemployment and rich people. I am not political you understand but only an engineer. But it is a worry…Everything is a worry."

His words trailed off and his eyes rested on the empty glass. They decided the man was not seeking a free session and ordered another round.

"How are you finding life here?" enquired John.

"My friend, it's like a different world, a completely different world," came the distant, subdued answer as Jesus looked ahead of him, shaking his head. "I had hoped when I came here that there would be a life of equals here, but the prejudice against me is great."

"On what grounds?" asked Tom.

"Look at my skin and face. I am different, and there are racists here, big ones that let you know you are not welcome and…"

While Jesus was explaining his problems John had happened to look behind him and saw a heavily built man at the bar, leaning over and listening to their conversation. From the look on his face, there was no doubt he understood what was being said and his upper lip was curled in disdain. The Columbian followed John's backward gaze and saw the man and stood and confronted him.

"Why are you listening to us? *Why*? Are you English?"

"Why? Are *you* telling me I cannot listen to a conversation in *my* own country?" came the answer from the man in clear English. "Yes, I am Russian, but are you daring to say I cannot listen? Who are *you*?"

The Columbian looked at John and Tom and said hurriedly: "I am your friend, please excuse me; I see someone I need to talk to on the other side."

Before they could reply, Jesus walked away to join a group of people at the far end of the bar who had all the looks of fellow Hispanic students. The man who challenged him looked down at Tom and John and smirked. "Silly man. Almost dark as a nigger, but he couldn't even make that. Don't worry. His type are known here, and we try and keep them away from our girls…Well, the ones who are worth protecting."

He was going to carry on but was joined by two young men who looked surprisingly well dressed and from the richness of the aroma, were smoking Havana cigars. After a few loud words and laughter, one gazed down at the Englishmen and enquired loudly: "Fancy two women? We have good choices. One has just arrived from Kazakhstan and promises she's a virgin."

"Yeah, she says her mother is a virgin as well," joked the other. "So, wanna try her too?"

The coach travelled slowly around the town centre on a gloriously clear morning as Dina explained Minsk's history.

The travellers tried to comprehend the violent past as she recounted it in her lilting, softly spoken English. Unlike the guide in Berlin who rammed home the atrocities of what had happened, the understated voice added to the tragedy of what had occurred all around them.

Along this street, she explained, hundreds were mowed down by the SS; up against that wall, mothers and children failed to escape the bullets aimed at them. Here in what was a shelter for children, grenades were hurled down and the doors closed as the explosions and cries of horror and death resounded. The group listened silently, astounded by the sufferings of the people in the area, including Rick.

"My God!" he exclaimed, looking at Tom and John. "Can you believe all this? We never got it mentioned in our history books on the war."

"Did your history books ever go outside the Florida Keys?" chided Tom.

"Only when we saved your butts twice this century, smart arse," replied Rick, smiling and adding: "Love you too, Tommy."

Dina resumed her commentary and when asked, said that the huge red words draping the buildings urged the people to work harder for a better future. "You see, we are in the Soviet Union, the first workers' state in the world and we must work hard to preserve it. We have strived against enormous odds – war, hardships and outside aggression. But we have a society that has come through all these drawbacks. That is why we have no problems with crime, racism and prostitution and…"

"But we were asked to buy two girls last night!" shouted John.

There was a momentary silence and then came the frosty reply: "Then these were crazy girls, and they were after your hard currency."

"So, it was our fault?" pressed John.

"I will talk to you later about this, sir," came the answer, and Dina pressed on with the story of Minsk.

They had time to stop at the central park and got out to see that here at least was a haven from the massive buildings and wide roads. They gathered around a simple fountain that offered the more professional photographers some good shots of the statues there against the sun that would help with the right angles, make water turn into shiny droplets.

John wandered with his camera further until he came to a spot where a memorial was being attended to by young people dressed in the Pioneer[31] uniform he had seen before. In front of the memorial burned a flame that he understood was to the fallen and victims in the Great Patriotic War[32], and he stood behind it, watching the young people lining up.

At the centre was a pretty girl in her mid-teens who was making sure the youngsters beside her were together properly to pay their respects. Silence fell and John was tempted to take a photograph, focusing on the girl's concentrated face, where she was standing apparently wrapped lightly by the flickering flame. He was too embarrassed to take the step of snapping her in case it destroyed this brief period of reflection. The moment passed and the group bowed slightly and moved away.

"And after this, you had to ask me about women you could have bought for a few dollars?"

By his side was Dina, and he caught his breath and kept his gaze on the flame.

"Did it amuse you to see a few poor girls in the hotel bar who can be bought? Don't you see them all the time in the West? *Everywhere*?"

"My apologies if I seemed uncaring, but it was you who said you had no problems with crime or prostitution, not me. And how would you know when Brezhnev stopped publishing the crime figures some years ago?"

"Who lives here in this country every day? You or me?"

He turned to face her and was staggered by how her face was so saddened by his words. Her expression was like that of a parent badly failed by her favourite child.

"Sir, I asked Louis your name, and he told me you are a good man. So, John, our society is not perfect, and we have people who can be good or bad, but you are here on the second day in the Soviet Union…and you can judge us like this? If I came to Britain and said the same, what would you think of me?"

"Oh, at the moment, I would say you would be very right if you judged us poorly," he answered, cagily. "We're well down the road of exploiting people, and it'll get worse. But I suppose when I came here, it was a feeling that such ways would not be tolerated. Last night, we experienced the shock of a Columbian student telling us about how he was being treated here. We then got the surprise of being offered buying women in the Soviet Union. Please forgive my naivety."

"We may not be as open as you, but I get to think that sometimes that might not be too bad, don't you think?" asked Dina as the Englishman played awkwardly with his camera and strap. "Look how happy we would be if Adam had not eaten the forbidden fruit in the Garden of Eden…Or if there had been just a minor chromosome difference, we had Adolpha Hitler, the dutiful Austrian *hausfrau*. Instead, we have memorials like this all over our country and the rest of the world to what the monster came and did…"

Dina let her words trail off and pointed to where she could see the awaiting travellers by the coach in the distance. She smiled as they walked along and calmly stated: "I have a feeling you may ask some questions I don't often get as an Intourist guide. I hope I am able to provide you with the answers you think are honest and satisfactory enough."

Chapter Nine

With a long drive of over 400 miles from Minsk to Moscow on the M1 highway, Arnaud kept the coach going as long and as far as he could. They had already driven through the stunning Białowieża Forest that straddled Poland and Belorussia, so this part of the journey was less impressive.

Inevitably, the need for comfort breaks arose, and on one of them, the driver realised that the coach was short of diesel. He was by the vehicle having a cigarette and looking down the empty road, shaking his head and mumbling to Martine, his now constant companion, giving a short wave as John approached.

"Will we ever see St Basil's?" asked John.

The Belgian looked at him and smiled but kept shaking his head while Martine wandered off.

"John, this is a bugger of a country to travel in. Western vehicles have to have vouchers to exchange at certain petrol stations. The last one wouldn't accept mine, and I don't know if we'll make the next one."

"What will you do?"

"Get you all together and have one almighty fucking prayer to St Basil. If that fails, dance naked in the forest and have an orgy to forget our problems. Rick and your mate will be up for that. Don't worry, friend, we have ways of getting help from funny places."

John walked on and came to Rick, for once alone and looking around him at some imposing oak trees lining the road on both sides. He asked whether the American was finding what they had already seen of the Białowieża Forest with its conifers and broadleaved trees, of particular beauty.

"Nope, just wondering what the lumber would fetch on the open market. You could make a fortune in this country if the commies would let you. Maybe some are already but keeping it among the commissars."

"I saw you chatting with a woman last evening in Minsk," noted John, and he saw an instant surprise from the American.

"My, your guy said you were a hack and now I can see why. She was no tom, just looking for help with something around the corner. Good English too."

"And the woman in the nightclub?"

"Well, now, she was a tom. Can you believe a university student needing the basics in life, and she was ready to do a blow job in my room for it? Even here, I don't do the full act, not with anything you get now. Heard about our AIDS with the gays and junkies? Lord, they were going mad for male pussy on the West Coast and never thought what they were letting themselves in for. Know how you separate the men from the boys in San Francisco?"

"Afraid I don't, Rick."

"With a crowbar!"

John decided to end the all too revealing conversation and walked on in search of Tom and spotted him by a tree with Harold Potter and Miss Clay. He stopped in his tracks and surveyed the sight of them surrounded by a glorious carpet of wild flowers. If he had never known them, he would have bet his life savings that he was the witness of a convivial meeting of son and parents. Their glasses were continually pushed back by them to stop them dropping off almost at the same time or wiped carefully. Both Harold and Tom had identical Panama hats, which they took off simultaneously to wipe their brows.

John joined them just as the talk took a turn that warned him to brace himself for the conversation.

"You'll never believe it, John, but both Harold and Carmen are cricket fans!" declared an exuberant Tom. "At last, people on my own wavelength."

"And guaranteed not to lead you astray, unlike others, young man," assured Harold, beaming at Tom. "One feels that if the Soviet Union could be criticised for one thing, it is not to have had the time to embrace the leather on willow game. Ah, to have had Boris driving a Wes Hall[33] delivery for six at the Moscow Oval. Or Ivan throwing a ball 30 yards to run out Beefy Botham[34] at Leningrad Lord's…Oh, dear, perhaps not that. But what a prospect!"

"I suppose it wasn't regarded as a game for the proletariat," remarked John, attempting to stifle a yawn.

"But there you're wrong," corrected Harold. "Look at the way it's been adopted by the working classes in West Indies, India and elsewhere. Nothing of the class-ridden game back home, what?"

The final expression and accent made John consider his response. Posh lefties who had invariably gone to private schools had always left him doubting.

While they had lambasted the capitalist system and exploitation of the workers, they had benefited from some of the privileges. They had also seemed squeamish when sitting in a working-class pub and listening to the expression of less than progressive views.

"I suppose I was rather harsh on the Polish chappie the other day, but it really gets my goat when they run down this wonderful place," he said, throwing open both arms.

"You feel you have seen the future and it works[35]…except in public lavatories?" said John.

"Do you know, I feel someone wants to lead me into a little trap with that amended quote," came the gently admonishing reply with accompanying wagging, spindly finger. "I left the Communist Party in 1956 over Hungary[36] and after '68 knew a terrible thing had happened, John. It was that the Party had forgotten it was there to lift up and defend the people. Instead, just like that crypto fascist, W.B. Yeats[37] warned in his poem, *The Great Day*:

"Hurrah for revolution and more cannon-shot!

A beggar upon horseback lashes a beggar on foot.

Hurrah for revolution and cannon come again!

The beggars have changed places, but the lash goes on."

"I remember reading that at school and always thought whoever made the lash, made the money," observed John. "Tom here as a Liberal believes that if the lash can be made ethically, all turns out well in the end."

"Listen, Murphy, the Liberal Party has never been one for mass purges," corrected Tom.

"Bit of an oxymoron for them, what?" queried an amused Harold to John. "In the first place, you have to get the mass to have the purge!"

"Oh, blast it! Last year, the Alliance[38] came within an inch of beating Labour into second, sir!" bellowed a reproachful Tom, causing some groups of travellers to turn and stare and Carmen to wince at the harsh words and hold her hand to her cheek.

"My sincere apologies, dear Thomas, I seem to have bowled you a nasty beamer[39]," replied Harold, bowing as far as his rheumatism would allow and focusing on the ground below him. "Oh, I say what wonderful examples of forest fauna one gets from eating humble pie," he added, staring at the colourful flowers. "I do believe this is a sumptuous example of *Ranunculaceae*. Er, will someone be so kind to help me straighten myself?"

As if from nowhere, Pip bounded to Harold's side and helped the old man come back to a vertical position, at the same time scowling at Tom and declaring with disgust: "Jeez, are you proud of yourself? Pick on someone your own size next time!"

Tom looked around in horror at the groups who were viewing him with a mixture of disdain and contempt. He gaped at John who was about to offer his friend some comfort or support when aid came from the crusty botanist who smiled at the Australian.

"Very kind, young man, but young Thomas *is* my size," stated Harold. "I really deserved his opprobrium on the matter. So," he continued, looking around him at the fellow travellers, "let that be the last said on the matter, what?"

Tom's relief was brief as Joan glided by him, stopped and whispered: "You're neither a croc nor a koala, mate, just a smelly dingo."

He watched the woman march on, his lips moving but no sound coming from him as the damnation sunk in. John gave him an awkward hug and tried to lessen the damage to his battered ego, but nothing that he could say was going to help.

Instead, his eyes searched for what was happening back at the coach and if anything was being done to get it moving. He saw Arnaud was in conversation with Dina and Louis, and between the nodding heads, it seemed a course of action had been agreed. The coach driver took some money from Louis, and with Dina, the two went on down the road. They let a few cars pass by them until a lorry came into sight, which they managed to stop when the Intourist guide stood resolutely and bravely in its path. The driver listened intently to her and then shook his head, followed by Arnaud offering some notes, followed by another shake of the head. The Belgian pulled out more notes that were offered to the reluctant man. Eventually, the driver nodded, took the money and the lorry approached the side of the coach. Arnaud rushed back, opened the hold and took a long hose and ran around to the other side to open the caps of the fuel tanks of the two vehicles.

The travellers waited for the signal that the operation was completed and Arnaud came around to them with a thumbs up and huge grin. "Good news! *Détente* and dollars have won the day, comrades!" he shouted, pointing ahead. "All aboard! Moscow awaits!"

As they both struggled on to the coach, Harold grunted to Thomas: "Who does the silly bugger think he is? Napoleon?"

Chapter Ten

Tom gazed down from the hotel window on the series of anonymous white tower blocks and gave a disappointed sigh.

Moscow wasn't quite what he expected – at least this part reminded him of Birmingham on a bad day, in fact, a very bad day. The drive into Moscow from the west side had shown the scale of the city, and as Dina quickly explained, the great struggle against the Nazis and an explosion of population after the war meant sacrifices had to be made and as with Minsk, making the sprawl aesthetically pleasing was not part of the plan.

All in all, the holiday had not been what he had expected or wanted. Berlin and Warsaw should have been remembered for other things than his various *faux pas*, and he had got used to females on the trip not finding him attractive. But the persistent comparisons with Woody Allen by the American were not welcome because he felt that he should be taken more seriously. He still had papers stored away of the good work he had done in Northern Ireland, but he felt he was now a laughing stock. This was not just with Rick but many of the other travellers too and being compared to a smelly dingo by Joan was the last straw. He accepted he was always going to be regarded as strange and aloof by many people but believed he was unfairly mocked by those whose intelligence was well below his own.

Tom glanced at a bottle of plum vodka he had bought in Warsaw that was precariously perched on the window sill and brought it closer to him. It was still about two-thirds full, and as John had thought it foul, the likelihood was Tom was going to finish it off for himself. Once his taste buds had been knocked senseless after the first sip, it tasted fine to him.

He was finding drink was becoming his best and constant companion these days, both after the dull weeks working in Whitehall and at home during the weekends. The visits to see his parents outside of London were the only occasions when he felt obliged to behave himself, especially as his mother was a strict teetotaller. It was only when she had gone to bed that father and son got out the whisky decanter and began enjoying themselves.

Tom looked at his watch and considered whether the plum vodka should be tried but then thought it was too early after the night before. Louis had offered the group the chance to see the Moscow State Circus and most had agreed. The Russians were still used to animals in many of the acts and the sight of a miserable looking bear on a bicycle and muzzled, left many of them cold. Less objectionable had been the dancing dogs but the lions' act resulted in the group feeling uncomfortable. They had returned to the hotel bar and hit the real vodka with too much gusto but were warned by Dina of an early start for the city tour via the metro.

The sound of his friend in the shower, singing an Irish rebel song at the top of voice was getting on his nerves.

"Well, some men fight for silver,
And some men fight for gold.
But the IRA is fighting for
The land that the Saxons stole."

"Must you sing that drivel?" asked Tom.

"What other drivel would you like?" replied his friend.

"Something that is not so objectionable."

"This Ireland of ours has for long been half free,
Six counties are under John Bull's tyranny.
And most of our leaders are greatly to blame
For shirking their part in the patriot game."

"Sometimes, Murphy, you…*you*…!"

All the travellers gathered around Dina after paying their five kopecks and as they investigated the Moscow Metro, marvelled at the spacious marble walls and stained glass windows.

Less welcome were the enormously deep and speedy escalators that whisked the passengers at what seemed twice the speed of those on the London Underground. For the travellers unsure on their feet, the others helped to lift them on to the steps. But they admitted a great plus was the complete absence of advertising along the walls.

As Tom wondered what to do, Rick grabbed him by the waist and placed him ahead with a roar that made the Muscovites stare. "Your turn on the way back, Limey!"

The sight of Tom turning and raising his fists mockingly to the American towering over him but with a glimmer of a smile, made even the most impassive Soviet citizens grin. "Hey, Ivan, I'm being mugged!" he shouted at one bewildered man.

Dina was full to overflowing with facts and figures for this undeniably impressive achievement that John felt outshone even the Paris Metro in grandiose scale and content. Her eyes were bright and voice tremulous as she recounted the history. When they came to the *Krásnaya plóshcha* stop, all were struck by the yellow marble arches that were overlaid with black Armenian marble. Paintings that had the appearance of religious depictions turned out to be of workers, peasants and intelligentsia, along with sculptures dotted around. It was no wonder that Dina proudly recited this particular station's appeal and even Rick was stunned by what he saw.

"Who needs to visit art galleries when you have this place?" he stated, slowly nodding his head in awe. "When these guys are allowed to let rip, they do it in style."

The group was led by Dina towards Red Square and again the travellers were impressed by the size but especially the chocolate box colours of St Basil's compared with the uniform brownish red of much of the Kremlin wall to the right, although there were golden onion domes poking above. Pointing out Lenin's Mausoleum and long queue snaking down from it, the guide suggested an early morning trip might be needed to see the revolutionary lying in state.

"Is it true he's made of plastic these days?" asked Rick, squinting at the line of people. "It's a long wait to see rubber blubber."

"Would you show some respect?" hissed Harold, who came close to the American. "For all that's holy, why should we do anything else than spit on the Lincoln Memorial like you're doing now?"

"At least he freed the slaves, buddy," said Rick with a smile. "Your guy set up the Gulag[40] for Stalin[41] to fill, isn't that so?"

"And, dear travellers, to your left here is the famous GUM[42] store that you are welcome to visit," said Dina, deliberately ignoring the spat developing before her. "You are free to wander around for the next two hours until those who wish to can come with me to visit the Exhibition of Achievements of the National Economy."

Harold turned around to Rick and, almost standing on tiptoe, declared: "There, will you be open minded enough to come to see the achievements in this park?"

"Why, when I can see real achievements in my own park?" answered Rick, beginning to move away.

"And what park could that possibly be?" sneered Harold.

"The good ol' park of the US of A."

With that and a cursory wave, the American strode away, followed by the baleful gaze of the enraged botanist.

"He really is the most arrogant, detestable of men!"

The outburst came not from Harold but Carmen and she shook her fist at the disappearing American who was still visible with his height and distinguished shock of white hair.

"There, there, Miss Clay, we must not let the day be ruined by the likes of him," comforted Harold with a gentle tap on her hand. He looked at John and Tom with an embarrassed smile.

"You must really forgive this, um, aggressive outburst from the two of us, but that man really is the most conceited person I think I've ever met. Now, on a more pleasant note, will you two be coming to the park with us?"

Tom nodded, but John gave a brusque shake of the head, which caused both Harold and Carmen to raise their eyebrows.

"I'd rather have a wander and see something else. They must have some bars around here, you'd think, but I've not spotted one. It's just a shame to come all this way and not really get to meet the people and relax. Think it's going to be a bit like Minsk."

Dina came up to him and asked if he would join the group and hearing his reply, tut-tutted. "That's a shame because I wanted to have more chats with you. I can't tonight because I have to go home this evening to see my child and husband. But we'll have our time later, maybe in Leningrad. I believe you've a more open mind than Mr McCoy."

"Even Ronald Reagan would have," he assured her. "I can't say that of Thatcher."

"Not a great supporter?" noted Dina. "She's very anti-Communist."

"But she hates *all* things socialist, Dina, even when they work. Maybe *especially* when they work."

He watched the group follow Dina back to the metro station and looked around him, deciding on a visit to the GUM store first. Visually, the building appeared a beguiling treat for shoppers with little bridges across the shopping areas, but as he investigated, John realised many of the goods on display were cheaply made but this did not stop queues for the most popular areas.

From there, he walked across to Lenin's mausoleum and took some shots of the exterior and the changing of the guard that was done with immaculate precision, notably the slow stepping of the soldiers timed to arrive just as the clock struck on the hour.

Of more interest to him was the procession of wedding couples who came to lay some flowers at the foot of the mausoleum, and with a few nods and *spasebas*, he was able to take snaps of the parties. All obediently gathered closely together while he photographed them. One of the brides looked at him and gave a tired smile. Perhaps a wild night of celebrations, but then he saw a slight bulge in her stomach and put it down to a little nausea in the morning. The clothes of both the men and women seemed dated compared with those in the West, but he was satisfied with the shots he had taken and the polite waves and nods he got as a stranger.

"Excuse me but I wonder if you could be kind enough to help me?"

John looked around and standing beside him was a young woman who leaned forward with an anxious face. She was in her twenties and very thin with a dark, long skirt and white 'v' neck blouse. He was drawn to how pale she was and how her big eyes matched the lack of colour in her face.

"I…I'm very sorry. No Russian. *Nyet* Russian, actually," he apologised, his arms raised with a shrug of the shoulders.

The woman smiled back at him and showed her hand, which he shook.

"Please don't apologise, I wouldn't expect you to," she replied in slow but good English. "My name is Vera. I'm a student."

"Hello, I'm John and a tourist from England."

"Where in England?"

"London."

"Oh, I would so like to visit!"

Her apparent enthusiasm was, on the surface, genuine, but these days John was cautious of being drawn into the unexpected, and he told himself to keep matters on a cordial level. He was tempted to see how her dancing was if the opportunity arose. The sight of flashing eyes would be his cue for an immediate exit.

"But I am afraid it is impossible," continued Vera. "Ordinary people can't go. Too expensive and unless you are an artist or sportsman, going to the West is very difficult."

"Or maybe a Party member?" asked John.

"Yes, there are advantages," she confirmed, sighing, "but I am not a communist, so only in my dreams will I ever see London."

For a moment, the two stood in silence while the wedding couples came to place their modest bouquets of flowers. John wondered what to do as Vera waited for him to continue with the conversation. He fumbled with the camera and looked around him.

"I wonder if you'd like to join me for lunch?" he blurted out, and she nodded quickly to the suggestion. "Er, but where I have no idea."

"Thank you, John, I know a place very near." And she began to walk with him following obediently as they crossed Red Square and went towards the old Metropol Hotel. "There is a little café I know which is not very expensive and we can have lunch there."

The waiter handed them the menus, which were entirely in Russian and John asked Vera to choose for them, requesting a beer while she opted for a mineral water.

This was hardly a little café, he decided as they were in a grand looking room. The huge windows were draped with heavy, dark yellow curtains, and the waiters were scurrying by, wearing outfits more suitable for a high class Parisian salon. John was surprised how busy it was with conservatively dressed people who were speaking in a restrained manner. Not quite a gentlemen's club, he concluded but remarkably similar.

He wanted to take the opportunity to ask about her life in the hope of finding how it differed from the West. However, her answers, though courteous, revealed very little except that she had decided to stay with her parents while she studied chemistry at Moscow University. Most of her time was devoted to her studies, but she went out occasionally with friends to the cinema, especially when the latest Tarkovsky[43] film was released. Her eyes became sad as she played with the serviette.

"It's a shame," she muttered.

"What is? You mean his latest film is difficult to see, or it's not been released?"

"Sometimes a film or a novel can be very hard to see in my country."

"Is that what you think of someone like Solzhenitsyn[44]?"

The name made Vera look elsewhere and she said quietly, "We can read him when we can get copies…unofficially. Oh, the service is very slow here!"

She took a book from her bag and flicked through it and smiled as her eyes alighted on the word she was looking for and nodded her head, smiling at John.

"You see, this is my Russian-English dictionary, and I was not too sure if I ordered the right meal for us. What a strange word you use…We say *iznezhennykh*…and you say, 'coddled'. I like this word of yours, John. Do you know why? Because it's so like 'cuddled', isn't it?" She giggled, now with sparkling eyes. "Have you ever cuddled an egg?"

To see her animated, happy face made him realise this was not the time to go into any depth about politics or serious matters but to enjoy this innocent moment, and he nodded as the waiter delivered the eggs in two small metal containers, covered in bubbling cheese with some ham poking out. A little green salad was put by the coddled eggs, and they began to tuck in.

"John, I have a favour to ask you."

John looked up and saw Vera's pale eyes staring back at him as she finished off her meal and dabbed the serviette around her lips, clearing her throat and composing herself. He thought there had to be a reason why he was picked out in the crowd buzzing around Red Square, and he braced himself for the request. Something outlandish? Was it to be money, maybe for services yet to be rendered?

"I need a tape recorder for my studies, John, and you see, the Soviet ones are so poor. They sometimes have bad sound and then they stop working. Would you be kind and help me get one from a shop that sells good ones?"

He began to relax as all the thoughts that she was a mercenary woman after his western currency receded.

"What it will cost I will give you back in roubles. You see this shop will only accept western currency."

"A *Beriozka* shop?" he queried and she nodded.

"It isn't far from here. We can take the Metro. Thank you so much, John."

As the two moved near to the impressive walled Novodevichy Convent[45], John took stock of the trademark onion domes within.

They had been told by Dina that many of the churches in the Soviet Union were not 'functioning' and had been turned into other uses. But try as they might, the communist regime had not been able to eradicate everything from pre-Revolutionary times. Noting his interest, Vera gave a potted history of the Convent as she directed him towards an anonymous shop entrance.

Just as he was about to follow her, he looked to his left and in the distance saw someone who looked strikingly like Rick, talking with a young man. He tried to get another view, but a lorry blocked his vision and when it had passed, there was no one there to see. John thought it may have been his imagination and heard Vera asking him to follow her into the shop.

As they went past the doorway, a shout went out from an assistant behind a counter: *"Russians aren't allowed here!"*[46]

Vera kept her stare ahead and walked on quickly with John trailing in her wake, and she told him what was said. No one had barred his entrance into Harrods, he thought; only too light a wallet had blocked his way.

"She thinks by the looks of me I'm too poor to justify being here," she explained.

They mounted a flight of stairs to where the electronics goods were, and after a few minutes, she pointed to a Sharp tape recorder and asked John what he thought. He replied that the brand was well known and regarded highly in England, and she enquired whether the price was a good one for him. He nodded and took his credit card out when he saw the signs showed that all the usual ones were accepted.

"You know, with this recorder you could buy a Soviet car?" she stated with a sardonic smile and sniggered at his raised eyebrows and open mouth.

As he was about to pay for the recorder, Vera requested he wait until she went to another part of the store, and he looked at the other goods on display, noting they would be found in many of the top shops in London. A tap on the shoulder and he turned to see Vera holding up a white bra with a pleading look.

"We have no such ones in our normal shops," she explained, almost apologetically.

He wondered if he had been chosen to fit out her wardrobe as well as help in her studies but agreed, surprised when the amount charged for the two items came to 60 roubles.

"That's £60 in sterling," he noted, signing the chit and looking doubtfully at her.

"I promise I have it in cash for you but not here. On the way back to your hotel."

They were silent for most of the trip back to the hotel, and John wondered what next was likely to occur with Vera. He expected that she would pay him, but the thought occurred again, would it be the case that she would offer a payment in kind instead? Occasionally, he looked sideways at her as she sat prim and upright, and he dismissed the idea that she was the type to supplement her student grant in this way.

"Here, John, is my name and address and maybe we could be pen pals?"

She took out another piece of paper and offered it to him with her biro, and he quickly wrote his details for her but believed he would hear no more when he returned to England.

As they walked towards the massive hotel ahead, he noticed her open her handbag, take out rouble notes and quickly hand them to him without lessening her stride.

"I can't come in the hotel; they don't let Russians in," she said flatly, stopping and facing him. "It's the way it is. I'm sorry. I would like to come and have a drink with you, but unless I am *that* kind of girl and bribe them at the door, they won't."

He mumbled a goodbye and shook her hand, and Vera thanked him again for helping with her studies, but then she added, her eyes ablaze: "When I wear this bra, I will think of you!"

Chapter Eleven

The pianist in the hotel bar completed his first half performance and was wildly applauded by a group of Italian students who were celebrating the end of their studies in Moscow.

While their whoops of joy were dying down, Tom explained he had promised to keep it a secret but try as he might, he couldn't help but blurt it out to Rick as they knocked back another beer.

"Yes, it's John's birthday tomorrow, and I've been sworn to secrecy," he confided. "I told him: 'Don't worry, my lips are sealed.'"

"Well, you're a buddy that lives by his word," commented Rick, lifting the ice-cold beer, gulping down the contents and wiping his lips. "I hope that he had a better time wherever he went this afternoon than you did in that God forsaken park."

As he said the words, he heard tut-tutting behind him and without looking around, he declared: "Well, we're not going potty over what Yuri[47] did in space, and he didn't get nowhere near the Moon, did he? He didn't plant no hammer and sickle flag before our boys got there with the stars and stripes[48]! America does no sprint but the long game."

Rick watched as the cause of the tut-tutting came into view, and Harold maintained a fuming countenance as he bellowed: "Let me tell you that in October 1961 I was privileged to join the other crowds in Hammersmith Broadway and cheer Yuri Gagarin in his open top car."

"What car was that? A Lada?"

Rick watched as Harold's face blushed, realised there was a sense of embarrassment from the botanist and decided to go in for the kill.

"Don't tell me the East Germans loaned him an open top Trabant?"

"Er, no, the vehicle was, er, loaned by the British government, I believe."

"You mean an open top Mini?"

"Not quite," mumbled Harold and his reply became inaudible. "A...um, Rolls Royce."

"Oh, *oh*!"

"Is something wrong?"

The concerned question came from Dina who was in company with the elderly Australian women. She was about to leave to return to her home in the Moscow suburbs for the evening but heard Rick's exclamation and mistook it for some discomfort by the American. When Rick saw Dina coming, he knew it was showtime.

"I have a pain in my butt, lady," he replied, showing Dina where the origin of his pain was by raising himself slightly from the chair and pointing.

"Perhaps it's caused from the verbal diarrhoea you constantly come out with?" suggested Harold, rocking back on his heels. "I believe it's a pervasive condition in your nation and in many cases, incurable."

"If you weren't speaking like an English gent, you'd be on your way to pushing up daisies by now," growled Rick, standing and towering over his tiny adversary. "But because you speak in that civilised way, I'm going to give you the benefit of the doubt. The reason why, lady, I'm like this is I just heard your cosmonaut guy, Yuri, got taken around London in a big Rolls Royce. What is it with you commies and swanky cars?"

"I am sorry, but how do you mean?" asked a bemused Dina, stepping back from Rick a little.

"I'll tell you, dearie," began the Dame Edna lookalike. "We went to a museum today and saw Lenin's black Rolls Royce. Not a Zil[49] but a bloody Rolls Royce. How revolutionary was that?"

"We requisitioned the property of the bourgeoise and aristocrats, dear lady, after the revolution."

"Sure, honey, and guess who did the best requisitioning of all?" asked Rick, warming to the lively debate. "Old Vlad and the rest of his gang. Christ! I'm from the land of the capitalists, but sure as hell, we can buy four wheels when we want them, not steal them! Unless you're a thief, you work to get your car."

"Did Henry Ford work on the assembly line to get his?"

The question made them all turn and see Carmen with her hands clenched tightly together so that her blue veins stood out further on her wrinkly hands.

"Why, no, I guess not, ma'am," responded Rick, momentarily thrown by this intervention. "But sure as hell he gave them work, didn't he? And they didn't have to wait years to get cars like here."

"And another thing, what's all this I hear about the Zil lanes[50] for the Party bosses?" pressed Dame Edna, tapping her finger on Dina's arm. "While you comrades are caught up in the traffic, the commissars whizz by."

"Remember *Animal Farm*[51]," Tom said, joining the conversation, the beer beginning to have its usual impact. "Just remember about the pigs. Never forget about the pigs…Poor old Snowball…Or indeed the horses and donkeys."

"Are you talking about our *kolkhozes*[52] now, sir?" asked Dina, becoming more confused by the whole discussion.

"I have always seen myself as a Winston…"

"…Now hold on, pal, let's not get carried away with you being another…"

"…Winston Smith[53]," carried on Tom, oblivious to Rick's interruption and beginning to hiccup. "Although I have never been particularly afraid of rats, I would not have been averse to keeping one as a pet while a child. My parents were rather worried about bites. Not of me on the rat but, rather, the other way around. You know, by the way, as a civil servant in the Home Office, I would have seen nothing particularly demeaning about working in the Ministry of Truth[54]. Please excuse me for a while. Must find the little Room…101[55]. When I return, I will tell you how I can cut your taxes by a half. *Hah*!"

Tom rose from the chair and then sank back and eased himself up again to make a less than sure way towards the toilets and was watched by everyone, including Dame Edna who appeared to see his faltering movements resembling an uncertain toddler and its first steps.

"Dear possum, I may have been a bit harsh about him before…But I hope they broke the bloody mould after they made him."

Dina saw Tom disappear into the Ladies, tut-tutted and shook her head before noting him reappear behind a disapproving woman and sheepishly look at the group and point to the Gents with an awkward giggle.

"Mr McCoy, I wonder if you may help me?" asked Dina. "Mr Laurel appears to me to be a little drunk, and I have some details here of a booking for him and his friend for a meal to celebrate a birthday. I must return home now."

Rick nodded and took the piece of paper from her.

"It's for a very well-known Georgian restaurant called *Aragvi*."

"Hey, you have a good ol' eatery from Georgia?" exclaimed Rick with approval. "I just love their Brunswick stew!"

"No, no, Mr McCoy, this is our *Soviet* Georgia where the food is *really* good," corrected Dina. "But if they can't get in, I've also put down an Uzbek place called *Shurpa* not too far away. It has the best *plov*[56] you can imagine."

"You know I hate to say it, but your Russian food doesn't exactly tick my boxes," confessed Rick. "Now, I'm not expecting to see a McDonald's in Red Square or a Burger King by the Bolshoi but don't you reckon fast food joints might go down a treat here? Today, I went to some luxury place for lunch and ordered calves' liver in red wine. By the time it arrived, it had cirrhosis. Know what I mean?"

Dina listened to the joke without an expression and said icily: "Mr McCoy, I think you exaggerate. We don't have your consumer society, but then we don't have unemployment and the racism you seem to accept. We also had a war on our territory that killed millions. What did you have in comparison? Now, please excuse me."

Rick watched her silently as Dina nodded her head to the others in the group and walked determinedly away, stopping as Arnaud and Louis came into the bar and having some words with the coach driver. Louis continued to the bar and ordered a drink for himself and stayed at the counter.

The American looked sheepishly at the others who, in turn, regarded him with a mixture of surprise and disdain. He realised how badly his cheap joke had backfired and tried to think of something to lighten the mood as the pianist returned to open the second half with a rendition of *What Kind of Fool am I?*

"One wonders if anyone should know the lyrics to this number?" queried Harold, gazing about him and then settling his eyes on the squirming American.

"Okay, okay, the big mouth Yank did it again," admitted Rick, raising his hands. "Apologies for being an asshole, but then I come from a long line of them."

"One feels it might stretch forever into the distance, Mr McCoy," stated Carmen, shaking her head sorrowfully.

As he was about to answer, Rick saw Pip coming out of the toilet, beckoning him to join him. Mumbling his excuses, the American sauntered slowly over to the young man who he admired for his looks and conquests in a way an ageing former alpha male has to.

"Yeah?"

"Afraid your mate is in a bit of a state in there. He hit his head against the wall and is sitting looking sorry for himself and bleeding a bit. Sobbing a bit too."

"Have you cleaned him up a bit?"

"Jeez, I'm on holiday chasing and getting the sheilas, not nursing some weedy Pom," declared Pip, grunting and walking away.

Rick watched the Australian wander off and shook his head. He was in two minds to do the same, but with no sign of John, he decided to go into the Gents and see if he could get Tom in a fit state to take him to his room.

Despite the hotel being a class above the usual in Russia, the smell of urine was evident, and it was clear that the cleaners hadn't been there for a while. Rick failed to see Tom at first but then noticed one of the cubicle doors was closed.

"Hey, fellah, don't go and hide from your Uncle Rick now," he said out loud. "Let's get you spruced up for the night."

The door was unlocked, and Tom stumbled out, clutching a bloodied handkerchief to his forehead. He was trembling and a few tears were trickling down those sallow cheeks as he looked up at the American.

"So, you tested out a Russian wall and found it could take all that you could throw at it?"

"It's dark, and I misjudged where the exit was," explained Tom, feebly.

The American put his arm gently around the little civil servant, led him to a basin, took out his clean handkerchief, wetted it under tepid water and placed it over the gash, dabbing and taking a closer look.

"I…I…wonder if I might be turning into an alcoholic, Rick," confessed Tom, subdued and looking ahead at the wall mirror.

"'If' you're an alki, so what? You've got a good job that'll see you to retirement unless you do something stupid. Okay, I'll be brutal now; you're not God's gift to women but…so what? Many of them ain't God's gift to men too! If you get sozzled from time to time…or most of the time, who cares? You're no molester or serial killer. So, there we are, Tom; you're further up the pecking order than you think. Now, let's get you ready to face the world."

Tom found the words comforting and glanced again at the mirror but was shaken by what he saw. The face was drained except where his forehead was cut, but then he had been prone to have falls more recently when he had been drinking and his brow had often hit the pavement. Truth to tell, he seemed to be matching

Henry Cooper[57] in scar tissue above his eyebrows. He glanced up at Rick who was looking at the reflection too and observing him wryly.

"See, Tom, you're Scarface, but be Scarface with *some* attitude. Give me a growl."

Tom tried but it sounded a pathetic whimper, yet Rick playfully jumped back and cupped his hands to his ears.

"Wow! From here, I can hear the tumbling walls of Jericho!"

Chapter Twelve

The young Georgian waiter finished smoking his cigarette, shrugged his shoulders and looked again dismissively at the two Englishmen before him, one of whom was waving a piece of paper written by Dina concerning John's birthday booking at the *Aragvi* restaurant.

A colleague of his came out and accepted a cigarette from the other waiter and lit it, looking completely indifferent as he took the paper and read through it and shook his head.

"No name on our list. No meal here."

"But our Intourist guide phoned and got the booking," explained John. "I was there when she phoned."

"No booking made, go somewhere else," came the curt response from the waiter who handed back the paper to John. "You no eat here."

The waiters sucked on their cigarettes and spoke in Georgian and then flicked the fag ends into the street, ignoring the protests from the Englishmen who looked depressed at their treatment. John gazed in despair up and down the length of Tverskaya Street and muttered to himself.

"What a bloody great birthday!"

"Happy birthday to you, sir."

The greeting made was said in perfect English, and John and Tom turned and looked at a man in front of them who smiled back.

"What a terrible shame they won't let you in. You, you really are missing a great treat for your celebration. Let's see if I can persuade them."

The man was in his late sixties or early seventies, and he sounded a well-to-do Englishman who except for heavy spectacles, looked and moved younger than his age with a full head of hair and an air of confidence and authority. He approached the waiters who appeared to recognise him as he talked to them haltingly in Russian and they, in turn, nodded and spoke back to him in a tone that was full of a respect that had been absent for them. But when they listened to his request, they still shrugged their shoulders with one of them going inside.

"I have asked them to check once again to see if they have any cancellations to get you inside," explained the Englishman. "At…at least, I think I did. My Russian is really appalling. I can just about understand the menu. If you get in and you like dumplings, try the *khinkali*[58]. My favourite is *satsivi*, that's chicken in a walnut sauce, m…most delicious."

John noticed that although the man oozed self-confidence, he was just about controlling a stammer, and there was something about him that seemed familiar. Tom meanwhile was walking away towards the entrance and shaking his head, doubtful there would be any admittance to them.

"Your friend is impatient, but this is a country not known to excel when it comes to service. You know, once my wife and I tried to get a shop to give us a whole goose to cook, but the rules said we could only have a half of one. Lucky, very lucky my wife is very, very tenacious, and we got it!"

"He was hoping that we could have a memorable time for my birthday and this hasn't exactly come up to expectations. Not that the food has been memorable on this trip anyway. We've had tough steak twice a day with tinned vegetables. The free beer at the table is welcome though."

"Your b-birthday? Yes, yes, you said that already," said the man, clasping his hands tightly. "Oh, what is the Russian for 'birthday'? Er, *den'rozhdeniya*, is it? That might have swung it!"

"Have you been here for very long?" asked John.

"Oh, for years but I must admit that I have been lamentable at learning Russian. Married to my lovely Russian wife, you see, who's fluent in English. And I had a small circle of…f-friends."

"English too? You must have taken early retirement?" observed John, growing intrigued by the man before him who nodded slightly to the questions.

"Exactly, health reasons, you see. You do like asking questions, young man."

"It's what comes from being a journalist," replied John and noticed the man's smiling face freeze. "I'm not Fleet Street material, just a building press hack on holiday."

The warmth in the smile returned to the elderly man's eyes, and he looked at Tom who had decided to stare through the restaurant's window.

"And your friend? He has more, shall we say, of the curiosity of the Fourth Estate."

"No, a civil servant in the Home Office."

"Ah, in my time I had some personal experience of both professions," the man said with a twinkle in his eyes. "Plusses and minuses for both, although yours offered some jolly colourful moments."

One of the waiters reappeared and with Tom in close attendance, came towards them, again shrugging his shoulders as he approached.

"So sorry, Mr Sonny[59], so sorry," he began in English. "No table for these gentlemen. Only your table, no room for them."

The man called Sonny shook his head at the news and turned to Tom and John and shrugged apologetically, his lips twisted downwards to make clear how sorry he was. He put one hand up to the waiter.

"Oh, dear, but we must get these gentlemen to some alternative; it's this man's…b…birthday, after all." John took out the piece of paper, turned it and showed Sonny the name of the other restaurant, which the elderly man examined and squinted, looking around him.

"I do believe that is near to here," he declared, letting the waiter see it and receiving a nod. "A taxi should get you there. The waiter will hail you one and make sure the driver understands. I haven't visited the *Shurpa* myself, but I gather their *plov* is extremely good and spicy. You m-must excuse me if I depart now but time and tide waits for no man, even in the Soviet Union, and I'm quite famished."

He bowed stiffly to both of them and walked to the restaurant entrance, and they watched the door open as he approached and disappeared. John and Tom exchanged glances and then both shook their heads.

"It can't have been," remarked John, scratching his forehead.

"I hope not," replied Tom. "I'm here to be seduced by Russian blondes, not talking to a traitor. Whatever will my bosses say?"

"Maybe 'Better luck next time'?" queried John, only to be confronted with a familiar admonishing finger.

Before they could say anything more, they heard a high whistle from the Georgian waiter to them who was standing by a yellow Volga taxi and waving to them.

"You, come here! Come here! Hurry, Moscow taxi driver no wait for no one!"

Tom and John approached the taxi cautiously and looked closely at the taxi driver; a young, smiling face greeted them in a way they could never remember a black cab equivalent in London doing.

"I tell him – him called Pyotr – that you wanna *Shurpa* and that is all. He speak English better than me here."

The waiter held out his hand expectantly and Tom shook it and opened the rear door and got in, not seeing the scowl on the Georgian's face, while John clambered in the other side. He looked down at the taxi driver and muttered in his language: *"Shitty English jokers!"*

The taxi revved and then lurched down the road with the driver hunched over the wheel and talking to himself in Russian. The cab itself was decked out with icons on the dashboard mixed with satanic miniatures – a sight that made the travellers look at one another nervously.

"Er…The waiter said you speak English," began John.

"*Da*…How now brown cow…The rain in Spain stays mainly in the bloody plain…We shall fight them on the beaches…To be or not to be…but better the flight of the bumblebee!"

The taxi screeched to a halt at a red light, and the driver took a cassette tape, waved it at them and put it in the player.

"I got this from German tourist, and I like it. Know why? The commissars don't and wanna have only beetle[60] insects!"

Soon they were listening to a sound of an aircraft landing and familiar words filling the cab with Pyotr singing loud and out of tune, reaching a crescendo with the chorus:

Well the Ukraine girls really knock me out
They leave the west behind
And Moscow girls make me sing and shout
That Georgia's always on my my my my my my my my mind
Oh, come on
Hu hey hu, hey, ah, yeah
Yeah, yeah, yeah
I'm back in the USSR
You don't know how lucky you are, boys
Back in the USSR

"You found your Georgias here yet?" he asked, looking in the mirror and seeing the sorrowful shake of heads in the rear seats. "No? Where you go next?"

When he was told it was Leningrad, he nodded. "If you no get women there, you sign into monastery. Here your restaurant."

They pulled in front of the *Shurpa* but were concerned with the words under his breath from Pyotr.

"Maybe closed. I go see." He looked back at them and grinned. "You no run away. Know why? Child locks. I mobile Lubyanka[61]!"

"I'm not very happy with this, John."

"Oh, relax, will you? What do you think he can do with the two of us?"

"Just because they don't publish their crime figures, it doesn't mean there aren't any."

"And what do you reckon he's going to do with us? Sell us into slavery? Who in their right mind would want us anyway?"

"I'm just not very happy."

"Look, it's broad daylight. He's knocking on the door to see if it's open. Do you think he'd do that if he was going to kidnap us?"

"Maybe he has friends in there he's involved with."

"Well, let's hope they've had a bloody good meal! More than what I'm having for my birthday at the moment."

"One would think those satanic badges would make you disturbed about his nature."

"At the moment, the only thing that sets me shuddering is you going on and on."

"You may not be concerned about being another crime statistic, but I am."

"Well, no one will ever know because they don't publish them here, do they?"

Thomas gave a grumble and stared ahead at the taxi driver who was knocking persistently on the restaurant door until it was opened and a small little man poked his head out and entered into conversation. They saw Pyotr becoming animated and pointing towards them, followed by the other man twisting his head around and gazing in their direction. There was a shake of the head and the taxi driver listened attentively to what was said to him, his eyebrows shooting up and nodding his head. They noticed their driver looking furtively around him, followed by hurried whispers into the other man's ear before disappearing into the restaurant.

"I'm not very—"

"Yes, I know, Tom; you're worried how much you'll go for in the slave market, Spartacus."

"My name is not Spartacus, and I'd go for more than you, a limping Claudius."

"Bitch!"

Pyotr eventually emerged and walked slowly back to the taxi and raised his hands apologetically.

"Is closed, sorry, but I see way to celebrate your birthday. Take time but trip on me, not you. Okay?" he asked, pointing to himself. "Honest Moscow taxi driver is possible."

He got into the taxi and lit a cigarette and inhaled heavily before looking in his mirror at them.

"But I have to do favour for restaurant. They want meat for tonight, and I know place to get it. Then I get favour back. It's socialist way these days. You say 'barter', I think. Then maybe I take you to big party with my friends. You not forget it all your life."

John looked at Tom closely, fully expecting a shake of the head, but instead his friend was measuring the offer and smacked his lips.

"Well, normally, I would err on the side of caution, but as it's your birthday, I'll relent. But I say this to *you*, sir," added Tom, wagging his finger characteristically, "that any additional expenditure will come out of your pocket, not mine."

The taxi had made a quick dash across to the suburbs of Moscow with the driver insisting on putting on a tape of the Rolling Stones.

His rendition of *I Can't Get No Satisfaction* included him clapping his hands and pouting his lips like Mick Jagger while driving and cursing any cars crossing in front of him while continuing:

…When I'm drivin' in my car, and the man come on the radio
He's tellin' me more and more about some useless information
Supposed to fire my imagination…

It was obvious that this song was close to Pyotr's heart as he continued it, winding down his window and slowing the car to a snail's pace as he approached a group of girls and calling out to them before recommencing:

…When I'm ridin' round the world
And I'm doin' this and I'm signin' that
And I'm tryin' to make some girl, who tells me

Baby, better come back maybe next week
Can't you see I'm on a losing streak…

The women looked around, startled by the foreign words but seeing the good-natured smile on the man's face, giggled at one another as he bawled out, "I can't get no satisfaction!"

The driver's behaviour brought a smile to even Tom, and he glanced at John to show his approval.

The taxi carried on till they came to a non-descript back alley. A drab building with a sign that indicated it was some kind of wholesale butcher and processor. A number of staff in white and blue overalls were hanging around, smoking and joking. Before them was a Chaika[62] limousine and a tall man in a heavy moustache and a white suit who had started talking aggressively to them. It led to Pyotr, cursing in Russian and then turning back to the Englishmen.

"Some bloody Armenian wanting his order for his place. These lot from Caucasus big, big crooks! Big trouble if ever they get to West. Mafia like babies to compare, I tell you."

The Armenian puffed out his chest and cheeks and pushed at one of the staff, taking out his wallet and waving it at them. His cursing saw one of the staff scurrying away, and soon there were two others carrying heavy loads of carcasses and waiting for the man to open the car boot for them to load them into it. He looked around at the staff and sneered.

"You lot understand, I know big people and when I want, so do they. Get me what I want quick for next time or you lot will sweep streets…forever."

The sullen looks from the staff followed him until he got into the car next to a pale, heavily built woman with very black hair who stared ahead as his Chaika limousine drove off.

The staff watched it turn a corner, and then as one, they all exclaimed: *"Fuck you too, arsehole!"*

The taxi driver got out after the staff had calmed down and hailed them.

"Hey, don't swear like that at my brother!"

The workers turned around and on sight of him broke into laughter, and the women came up and hugged him like a long-lost son. A younger one held back until all the greetings were done and he turned to her, grinning.

"No greetings for me, sweetie?"

The woman was in her thirties and despite the drab uniform was attractive with brown hair and eyes and a pleasing figure. She rushed into his arms and gave him plenty of kisses. He looked back at Tom and John and said: "You stay there. Me and her go and check order."

After thirty minutes, Tom began tut-tutting.

"It can't take that long to sort out some meat, can it?"

"Soviet bureaucracy."

"It would never happen in Waitrose."

"Try the Co-op."

"That man's going to where they disappeared and opening the door and…Good Lord, I don't believe it…they are…!"

"…Could be wrong but they can't be brother and sister by the looks of it, Tom."

With one of her breasts partly exposed and being fondled, the moaning coupling continued with Pyotr's trousers by his ankles. The act was witnessed in awed silence as it continued and reached a climax with the other workers watching and giggling until the taxi driver and woman became aware they were being watched. He cursed and shut the door, giving them time to hoist trousers and skirt and emerge. The fellow workers said nothing with only the females smiling at the woman and the men nodding when Pyotr said a few words. He came to the taxi and looked in sheepishly.

"Sorry, sorry. Had to…to…sign papers. We get meat soon. Sorry."

As he said those words, he was unaware that he hadn't buttoned up his trousers properly and a semi-erect member made its greeting to further laughter from both the men and women workers. He turned and confronted them fully, scowling. *"What's so bloody funny, comrades?"*

One of the men pretended to lift binoculars to his eyes and moved his hands down in the direction while another man pointed.

"Is that the biggest sausage you have, Pyotr? We have bigger ones on sale here! Yours looks more like a chipolata."

The taxi driver followed the man's finger and gasped, quickly buttoning the trouser flies and shaking his fist at them.

"Yeah and I've heard there's more bog paper than meat in them!"

The accusation saw the two male workers looking at one another, the smiles disappearing quickly, and one of them stated coldly: *"One more joke like that and you can take your fucking sausage and stick it up your bum. You'll get no meat here for your Uzbek mates from us."*

The words had an immediate impact, and Pyotr put his hands up and approached them with a shrug of the shoulders, as he knew much was depending on delivering the meat to the restaurant.

"Oh, come on, mates, I stepped out of line and became like that Yerevan black. My apologies. Come on, you know me and my big mouth."

Pyotr put his arms around them both and said a few more apologetic words to pacify the resentment, eventually getting some nods. He pulled out of his shirt pocket what looked like small cigars and offered them to the men as a peace offering. They took them and waited for the taxi driver to light the cigars and watch the men savour their superior taste and strength. Pyotr pulled out another cigar and looked back at the Englishmen, eyes wide open and with thumbs up, he shouted: "Best Cuban cigars. Fidel Castro[63] smoke these…No CIA made…No explode!"

The farewell to the workers was brief, and there was no sign of Pyotr's lover as he revved up the engine and turned the taxi around.

Without a word to the Englishmen, Pyotr hunched over the steering wheel and accelerated, keeping an eye open for the police. Five minutes into the trip back to the *Shurpa*, they saw him begin to relax and hum to himself.

"Girl back there is very nice woman," he stated. "No bad whore. She very sad you saw her like that. Next time plenty flowers for her."

"We never thought she was bad," answered John. "You and she were just glad to see one another."

"We always glad, every time. *Magic*! You stay in Moscow I introduce you to her sister. For your mate" – and Pyotr looked in his mirror at Tom – "maybe their mother. But you no stay. Pity."

John saw Tom stiffen and become annoyed at the suggestion he should end up with what he imagined to be an ageing female at the end of the queue.

"Why should I be lumbered with a frumpy *babushka*?" he queried through gritted teeth, his grey eyes for once flashing in anger. "For God's sake! I have no intention of being seduced by any other than a desirable Russian blonde…as my superiors *expect* me to be."

"You wanna pay for a Russian blonde, I arrange," said Pyotr, "but she will want dollars. Better have *babushka*, my friend. Close eyes and think it's naughty Natasha…Oh, yes. Now hold tight, we go to *Shurpa* for deal and my pal there for his too."

The same screeching of brakes, cranking of gears and roar of the engine they experienced on the way to the wholesale butchers was repeated on the journey back to the restaurant. Pyotr laughed and joked to himself in Russian as he spotted Tom in the mirror blanching as some pedestrians went scuttling back to the pavement as the taxi sped by. At a red light, the taxi driver put in a tape and joined in with his off-key rendition of the Beatles' *Baby, You Can Drive My Car*, giving a toot on the horn when he saw a pretty girl walking by. He wound down the window and when it came to the second track on *Rubber Soul*, sang at a woman:

I once had a girl

Or should I say, she once had me!

"Are you coming to light my fire, sweetie?" he asked in English to the woman with a huge smile, while she looked back severely at him. He repeated the question in Russian.

"You dare to ask me and call me 'sweetie'?"

Her response caused Pyotr to look puzzled, and he shrugged his shoulders.

"Why not? Your luck might be in with me around."

The woman, who was in her thirties with swept back, dark hair, grey blouse and long skirt, snorted at the cheekiness and pulled from her bag a notepad and pen, walking to the front of the taxi and scribbling quickly the registration number before heading back. While she did the lights turned green and a few impatient tooting of car horns was heard.

"You are talking to a senior official of the Foreign Ministry in a disgraceful and disrespectful manner. I have taken your registration number, and I see now your taxi driver permit and have taken that down."

"Oh, comrade, please think. I am a poor man with family!"

"A taxi driver and poor? You must be a very mediocre one. But there is one way which I will forgive your insulting way with me."

"You have only to say, comrade. Whatever it is, I'll agree."

"I am glad to see you are contrite, comrade. I have a flight in the morning to Sofia, Bulgaria, from Sheremetyevo Airport at 2 pm. You will pick me up at 11 am…I am writing my address and telephone number. If you are late, you know the consequences? And this will of course be for free in light of me not taking the matter further?"

"Yes, yes, it will be my pleasure to drive you, comrade."

"Who are your passengers? They don't look Russian…"

"They're English. Not a word of Russian, thank God."

"Good afternoon, dear gentlemen," the woman said in perfect English. "I am sorry we have detained you on your journey. This kind taxi driver has offered to take me to the airport for tomorrow. Our Moscow taxi drivers are famous for their...yes, kindness and...generosity, are they not?" she asked Pyotr with a steely smile.

"Will be both tomorrow, comrade..."

"Good day, *sweet* driver!"

Taking the paper from the woman, he nodded and slammed his foot on the accelerator, only then cursing in Russian: *"Bring back fucking Tsar and be quick about it!"*

The back door to the restaurant was opened slightly to allow a nervous Uzbek man to poke his head out and see who the visitor was and having noted it was Pyotr, nodded eagerly.

In what seemed an instant, the taxi driver and Englishmen were ushered into the kitchen and a group of workers hurried out and swiftly brought in the large carcasses.

"Halal? Svinina?"

"He asked if there was pork," Pyotr explained to Tom and John. "If he thinks this meat is *halal*, he crazy."

"I no crazy," complained the Uzbek, surprising the taxi driver with his English. "I no ask, I no know."

The Uzbek looked at the Englishmen and made a courteous bow to each of them. He could have been in his thirties or older because his face was weathered, hair suspiciously dyed black, and when he smiled at them, there was almost a full set of dazzling gold teeth.

"Welcome, welcome. My name is Akmal. May I offer tea for you while we get meat in kitchen to start cook? Big bosses come from my republic. Must be fed or we get much pain. No cow balls, but our balls, oh yes. But we must have *plov* ready for bosses. You save our lives, Pyotr."

Akmal chuckled to himself at his gruesome, if inaccurate, prophecy as he went to the stove and prepared three bowls, pouring green tea into them from a flowery, blue pot. He presented them to Pyotr, Tom and John separately with his left hand, his right on his heart and watched them sip cautiously to begin with.

"Just making before you came," he explained, delighted to see them sip his tea with growing appreciation. Noticing how the noise in the kitchen was building up as the voices babbled, knives flashed and the saucepans were put on the cookers, the Englishmen could not fail to notice some mousetraps, two with unfortunate rodents lifeless in them.

"Not there long," said Akmal, following their looks and shrugging his shoulders. "No have rats yet. Pyotr, your friend in small room restaurant. I done funny-funny cakes for him."

Akmal picked up a heavy package and patted it, and they walked through the kitchen to a large and salubrious but faded room with two big hanging chandelier lights. The walls were partly covered by hanging carpets that had seen better days. The walls too were faded and chipped in places but still had impressive designs with arches that led to other parts of the bigger restaurant room.

They walked through a narrow door into a smaller, more modest room where a man was sitting with his back to them. As he turned, they could see he was far away from looking conventional for this part of the world. His long black hair was parted in the middle and was matched by dark clothes. His shirt was open and a heavy gold medallion almost covered his chest. When the man stood, he towered over them, giving them a sense that they were in the presence of an extraordinary character. It was only when he smiled at the sight of Pyotr that his charisma was challenged by yellow, cracked teeth, a discolouration that was probably down to heavy smoking if the packets of cigarettes by a full ashtray were any guide.

"Sasha!" exclaimed the taxi driver, giving the man a great hug. "My friends here are English-speaking; please can you speak in their language?"

"And why can't they speak to us in ours?" said the man raising his head, nostrils flaring at the foreigners before grinning. "No, no, welcome. I am glad to speak English with you."

He shook hands with John and then walked slowly around Tom with his right hand on his chin and a long index finger stroking his nose, while the Englishman stared impassively back. Sasha stopped and then grabbed Tom's shoulders firmly.

"We are in the presence of *him*! It is the great American director, Woody Allen, Pyotr!"

The two Russians came together and began discussing this apparent discovery in their own language, while Tom looked at John, smiled and put a finger to his lips. To his friend's amazement, it seemed Tom was uncharacteristically going to play along with his newfound fame.

Sasha broke away from Pyotr and came up to Tom, looking him up and down with admiration.

"And you are here in this restaurant...*You!* What brings you here to Moscow? Another film?"

Tom nodded.

"Will it be like what you call a sequel? To your *Love and Death*?"

Tom nodded again.

"What will you call it?"

"*Hate and Life*," said Tom after a moment's deliberation. "But I'm afraid, the regime here won't allow me to film it in Moscow, so I am on my way to Helsinki to see the sights...I mean, find suitable places for shooting the film."

Sasha nodded and tut-tutted at what he saw as a typical restriction by the regime.

"You know we have KGB coming down hard on our concerts[64]. They have opened places where rock bands can play but only to spy on us and our fans. So, we say *nyet* and play anywhere else we can. But you, Mr Woody, have to take your genius elsewhere than where it should be. My apologies for their tyranny, sir."

Tom nodded, modestly.

"I take kids of Party bosses to these KGB places...these Comrade cockroaches!" spat out Pyotr and gave Tom an unexpected hug. "But this master, he no get chance here for his art."

"I wish if you would honour me with your autograph, sir," requested Sasha, spotting a menu on a nearby table and taking out a biro. "Please, if you would sign. If you would mind to write: *Greetings to Sasha and the Mensheviks*[65] *from Woody Allen*. That's my band. Very dangerous name. Only use when we play our concerts, not theirs but then only when we have to."

"And when you play theirs?" queried Tom as he forged the film director's name.

"*Sasha and the Bolsheviks*," shrugged the musician. "We gotta live. Pyotr here says one of you has birthday today. Who? I have nice sweet cake here to give you some."

The two Englishmen looked at one another with a nod between them; Tom stepped forward and pointed to himself.

"Ah! You give me signature, so you have slice of this great cake cooked here in restaurant. Akmal!" shouted Sasha, clapping his hands. "Vodka to celebrate Mr Woody's birthday and you have food to give us soon?"

The Uzbek nodded quickly and scurried off while Sasha carefully took one of the cakes from the packaging and having spotted a knife on the table, made a large slice, presenting it to Tom.

"It is our honour, Mr Woody."

Tom smacked his lips and began to bite into the slice, appreciating the taste with a nod and smile as he began to devour it before them.

"John? It's rather good in a manner of speaking," said Tom, spluttering some of the cake before him. When he saw his friend shaking his head, he continued to finish off the remainder, picking up a serviette and dabbing his mouth with great satisfaction.

Akmal returned with a tray that had a full bottle of vodka and three tumblers, which he quickly filled and offered to his guests.

"A toast!" shouted Sasha and then cleared his throat: "May the years to come see more great films from you, dear Mr Woody and that you may come to Moscow and be free to make one here. *Na Zdorovie!* Cheers!"

Tom raised his glass and like Sasha, downed it in one, making John feel a little concerned how the rest of the day was likely to go.

"And may I, good sir, raise a glass to you too," insisted Tom, pouring vodka into their glasses and raising his. "To the time when your music will be heard everywhere in the Soviet Union! Cheers!"

"To Annie Hall and may she inspire you again!"

"To *Back in the USSR* sung by you and your band of Mensheviks, sir!"

"May you continue to have pleasure with that young beauty in *Manhattan* forever!"

"I will drink to that wish, if not command, sir! Where is she?"

As the toasts continued, it was obvious to John that it would not be long before he had to deal with Tom and the long road back to the hotel until he realised there was a strange look coming into his friend's reddening eyes and the smacking of his lips was even louder than usual.

"The rain in Spain stays mainly in the plain and is a decided pain! Why are we in sunny Iberia and not in Leningrad?"

"We are in Moscow, Tom," stated John, looking at Tom's wild eyes as his friend gaped at him.

"I realise that, Don José, or are you El Cid?"

"Tom, don't you think…?"

"Of course, I think, that is to say…I do in my waking hours but not so when I slumber. Perchance to dream, what? Why are the walls pressing closer to us? Are they members of the KGB because…because…*Shhhh! Shhhh!* My friends. *Beware!* We are in the land of mushroom gathering[66] and gulags."

Pyotr came close to John and whispered: "I think cake it kicks in sooner with vodka."

"Whispering? Whispering? I hear the whispers of viziers and assassins. *Et tu Brute*! A horse! A horse! My kingdom for I'm a Norse, of course and if I might say, getting quite hoarse…*Hah!*"

"Let's get him back to the hotel quick," insisted John, trying to grab Tom who fought off the friendly hand.

"This is not the end, this is not the end of the beginning, this is the middle, and I want to have a piddle! I've lost my manhood…who stole it? I had it in my trousers just a moment ago! Stop thief! Police!"

The taxi sped on as Pyotr and John in the front realised that the passenger in the back was becoming delirious.

"I want to know why St Peter's Basilica has grown onions!"

Pyotr squinted and noted: "He think we somewhere else."

"I grow old! I grow old! I shall wear the bottom of my trousers rolled!"

"Oh, Christ, he only starts reciting T.S. Eliot when he's blind drunk," observed John.

"Shall I compare thee to a summer's day, sweetie? I say, old boy, can I open the window and have a wank?"

"You're not in private school now. No you bloody can't."

"It's a free country, isn't it? Where's the Lincoln Memorial? God, I'm randy!"

The taxi halted outside the hotel and Pyotr sighed, blew out his cheeks and hunched over the driving wheel, looking askance at John.

"Sorry, so sorry, my friend for this. My fault. No charge, go and…He gone!"

The words made John turn around to see Tom had opened the door and was running into the hotel entrance with his shirt in one hand and close to a couple of security men who were negotiating entrance for two heavily made-up women with the shortest of miniskirts and plunging necklines.

"I want a pure Russian blonde!" shrieked Tom.

"Here! Here!" said one of the girls.

John came up to his friend and suggested he would be more likely to gain entrance to the hotel with his shirt on to which his friend agreed and looked at the women before giggling.

"You see, I am a famous American director called Woody Allen and if any of you ladies would like to join me on a casting couch…for an audition and consensual monkey business, what?…Stop pushing me, sir!"

The Italian students were gathered around the pianist as he played a number of light operetta numbers for them. They roared at the end of every piece as they chattered excitedly that they were going home the following day after their year in Moscow. There would be no more hunting, often vainly, for fresh fruit, and they could forget the sweet wines from Georgia for those of Chianti and Sicily.

But then in front of them came into the room the small but determined sight of Thomas, eyeing them and nodding sagaciously as they finished their singing of *Arrivederci Roma*. He tried to clap in time with the pianist with John shaking his head and looking forlornly at the amused faces of Arnaud, Martine and Rick.

"My brave, brave Muscovites!" exclaimed Tom, coming up to the bemused Italians and embracing them. "Remember, we don't have to be enemies; we can be friends!"

"Doesn't your buddy know they're from Milan?" asked Rick to John. "Hey, Woody! Wrong country!"

Tom swung around at the words, spotted Rick and waved a fist at the American, spitting out: "Watch it!"

Chapter Thirteen

The coach slowed and stopped on the bridge as Dina cleared her throat and brought the microphone close to her and stated in a heavier than usual accent: "Ladies and gentlemen, this below you is the mighty Volga River, which is the greatest in Europe and has played its part in the formation of the Russian people."

"Sure beats the hell out of Old Father Thames," whispered Rick to Tom and John with a smile and a wink. "But has it got the beating of my ol' Mississippi?"

"Ladies and gentlemen, the Volga is over 1,000 km more in length than the Missouri or Mississippi rivers in the United States," added Dina, looking directly at the American.

"Guess my voice carries further than I thought, guys," remarked Rick. "Or she really is in the KGB."

Dina carried on explaining the beauty of the area around the Volga, helped by a gloriously sunny day and then nodded to Louis, handing the microphone with him and approached the American who began to shift uneasily in his seat. He picked up a paperback entitled *How the West Will Win* and then recognised his mistake.

"Is this a book that reflects your views on us, Mr McCoy?"

"Well, now, I just like to get a wide range of them, Dina. You know, some years ago I bought a copy of Marx's *Kapital*."

"And what did you think of it and his critique of capitalism?"

"When I've read it, I'll let you know," said Rick with an appeasing smile.

Dina picked at the top of the seat before the American and hesitated to say anything more.

"You see, I'm just an ordinary guy, Dina, and not what you'd say, too savvy with affairs of the world," explained Rick. "I grew up in a country that gave me what I wanted without asking how things got there in the first place."

"So, if you knew that what you bought was off the back of workers exploited even in your own country, that would be acceptable?"

"Honey, they could stop being exploited by getting off their knees. We don't need no state telling us what to do and…"

Rick stopped as he heard Tom issue a large tut and saw a shake of the little man's head.

"Oh, come on, buster, since when can you limeys take the high ground with your empire?"

"We abolished the slave trade in 1807 and slavery in 1833 while you, sir, didn't match that until 1865," sneered Tom.

"Sure, because you'd got all of them you wanted, and they were breeding enough in the colonies!" retorted Rick. "By the way, asshole, how come if you were so generous, all the compensation went to the slave owners and none to the slaves?"

Dina was listening with increasing concern at the mounting argument between the tourists. She had been an Intourist guide for over two years now, and this trip had been the most strained. Her life at home had been a difficult one with her husband often absent and behaving distantly towards her. There were only two joys in her life – her son who was at an age where his wonder at the world around him made her optimistic that he would achieve much in his later life.

And then there was her job where she could meet foreigners from the west who had proved, for the most part, inquisitive without challenging her on the politics of her country too much. She had been warned about this aspect in her training but nothing had prepared her for the nature of the American's bombastic manner or the two Englishmen who in a quieter way, probed and tested her beliefs.

While the two were polite, Dina was finding the constant quips by John beginning to irritate her, especially his sarcastic remarks about the sameness of the meals on the trip while he and his friend greedily drank as much of the free bottled beer at the table. As a westerner, he probably did not know how more stressful it was to shop for food and other necessities in recent times. While prices were held at the same rate, good food was becoming scarce, even in Moscow. Fatty, gristly meat and very few sightings of butter in the shops, often led to arguments with her husband as well as scuffles in the queues. There were times when she had to resort to the black market; this was something she was reluctant about but which she accepted many were now being forced to.

She had also found the Australian women far too blunt for her taste, especially when they had criticised Lenin for driving about in a Rolls Royce. The other holidaymakers tended to blur into the anonymous types she was used to dealing with.

The two exceptions were Harold and Carmen who she found *very* English in a way she had been so amused by and recalled when she had read through Agatha Christie novels. She decided that Harold might make a passable Hastings had he been younger and taller, but Carmen was perfect for Miss Marple.

Arnaud and Louis had provided some light relief for her. The guide had become more openly effeminate in his gestures as the trip had progressed, and it was clear to her that unlike some of the others, she had nothing to fear from him. Arnaud was colourful in his own way and was more than ready to play to the audience. A smile appeared on her lips when she recalled how, when he said something to the travellers at the front of the coach and they applauded, he had stood by the side of the wheel and bowed with the coach still travelling.

Her smile faded as she gazed down at Rick and thought to herself how Americans on previous trips always seemed to complain if conditions in the Soviet Union were not exactly as they were back home. This one had been different, but there was little in his character that made her warm to either him or his country. While Russian men were often loud and obnoxious when they were drunk, Rick was just louder and more objectionable even when sober.

"When do we get to Leningrad?" he asked her, stifling a yawn and taking another slurp from Arnaud's Belgian beer.

"We are going to stop overnight in Novgorod, Mr McCoy," she replied.

"Oh, where's that when it's at home?"

"It's always at home, Mr McCoy," said Dina, with a gentle sarcasm. "It was a republic more than 500 years before your United States was formed. It offered much hope and culture to the people of the time."

"Well, maybe you'll get it back again if you follow the world's leading republic of today, honey," declared Rick, raising the beer can to her and failing to see the frown that sped quickly across the guide's face as she turned around and returned to the front of the coach.

"You could have treated her more respectfully, Rick," stated John, leaning over and wagging his finger at the American.

"You know, I think I could have," agreed Rick. "It's hard to be magnanimous when your nation's so great. And before you two get all uppity with me, remember how your mighty British Empire behaved when you were top slave owning dog. Oh, did I mention that before?"

The late afternoon light in the central park of Novgorod softened the look of the statues as the group split and went their separate ways.

John noticed two policemen who watched the westerners and saw them talk worriedly to one another. He thought it couldn't be they were going to keep them in one group, but when one shrugged his shoulders and shuffled off, he looked around to see where they could find a local bar. He convinced himself that this was the way to find the real Russians away from any expensive tourist traps.

Arnaud was ahead, walking with Martine and he looked behind and spotted the Englishmen, waving to them and stopping. The woman maintained her slow amble, smiling at the driver.

"You boys recovered from last night?" asked Arnaud, looking especially at Tom. "You looked very, *very* happy, my friend."

"I had been led to believe I was eating a birthday cake or something similar," explained Tom. "It turned out to be rather more exotic and, um, intoxicating than I thought."

"Mistaking Italians for Russians hinted at that," said John, winking at Arnaud. "How's Martine enjoying the trip?"

Arnaud nodded but then shook his head and looked glum and blew out his cheeks when he stated: "But problems, big problems with Dina."

"Well, I, for one, will defend your duty of care to us and ready supply of Belgian beer, sir," said Tom with a firm sweep of his hand. "And your driving has been immaculate, that is, first class."

Arnaud regarded the remark with a wry smile and glanced at John.

"That was some mighty strong cake," he commented, walking on to join Martine.

His remark about Dina made the two wonder that behind her smiling she was hard on the guide and driver in ways the tourists hadn't seen. John noticed, just after a very liquid lunch in Moscow with free beer, a hardness in her expression when he asked to take her photograph and she refused to smile.

As John walked away, searching for interesting shots to take with his camera, Tom looked around him and spotted Harold and Carmen inspecting the trees and flowers. The thought returned to him how many would think they must, by their looks and conversation, be his parents and a little smile played on his lips at the thought. Harold sensed his presence and straightened himself with difficulty, a grimace on his face.

"Oh! Oh! Never grow old, Thomas. It holds nothing to be recommended. I was just stopping Miss Clay from wandering around the park and looking at the statues to admire the beautiful flowers here."

"Well, I've been looking for some commemoration for one of the most famous sons of Novgorod, but there seems none at all," stated Carmen with a sorry shake of her head.

"And who would that be?" asked Tom. "Some warrior?"

"My goodness, no! If the Poles can have a statue for Chopin in their famous park, don't you think there could be one for Rachmaninov[67] here?"

"I'm afraid the powers that be might find him to be a rather reactionary figure, Carmen," suggested Harold, tut-tutting a little. "He left the country in a bit of a huff about the revolution after all. I'm sure they'll get around to building some memorial here."

By the pouting of her lips, it was clear that Carmen did not share the optimism, and she nodded brusquely, walking off and stopping at an enormous bell-like statue with bronze figures. Harold informed Tom that this was in memory to the great figures in Russia's past, from medieval times to the nineteenth century.

The two walked on with Harold humming a merry tune, stopping from time to time to admire some flora that meant nothing at all to his companion.

"Never been one to admire nature's wonders, Thomas?"

"I, that is, I suppose I'm rather ignorant on pastoral matters," confessed Tom, taking off his panama hat and wiping his brow at exactly the same time as Harold did. "We were never really brought up that way. Tents and climbing trees were never, well, *de rigueur* for us."

"'Us'? You have a sibling or two?"

"A sister. Kathy. We don't really talk. Bit of a falling out because of her getting married to a man who, well…I just think she could have done better. He's a *Sun* reader, you see."

"Good lord! So, if you don't mind me asking, Thomas, there has been some estrangement?"

Tom nodded and gave a little grunt as he recalled when he last visited his sister in Sheffield and the bad atmosphere throughout. The husband had sat with the television on or played punk music very loudly on his midi-system. Tom had tried making polite conversation but met a wall of sullen indifference, and when the visit was over, he decided never to go there again. Months went by without any contact with Kathy, and he had accepted that was the fate of their relationship.

"Were your parents aware of this?" probed Harold.

"Yes, but they are no longer alive," replied Tom, biting his lip. "They died last year."

"Oh, that is sad. Together?"

"My mother fell ill with cancer, and it was too much for my father, and he had a massive heart attack and died. We were never very close, you see but mother…mother…"

The nurse stopped Thomas going into his mother's room and explained that she had not had the best of days.

He admired the way she had suffered her illness with quiet fortitude, and the death of her husband had been borne with a similar attitude. He nodded quietly at what the nurse said and took a deep breath as he approached the room.

There was a sickly, almost sweet smell when he entered. As he approached her bed, he observed her fondly while she gazed vacantly through the window, picking slowly at the top of the blanket. A faint smile played across her thin lips, as she looked at two pigeons busy in a mating game on the window ledge. She heard his entrance and said rhetorically: "Silly birds; why bother?"

"Sorry, mother. What do you mean?"

She slowly turned her face to him, and he could see that her pallor was greyer than the last time, and her eyes seemed to have lost the usual sparkle.

"Hello, Thomas. All this dancing by the male and for what? It must remind you of those university discos you told me about. You trying to strut and impress but off those women flew. But these birds will just have a palaver of feeding those forever greedy mouths of their children."

Tom grimaced at his confession to her of his failure at the discos but put it to one side.

"Not that Stanley and I had any regrets with building our nest with you two," his mother continued, patting his outstretched hand. "Now, tell me your news."

He gave her a peck on the cheek and sat down and considered what he could say. The job was going relatively well, and he had settled himself down in the department, although he found it a bit dull after his time in Northern Ireland. After a short while, he found his conversation had dried up and looked at his mother who had shut her eyes during his talk and wondered if he should leave. But suddenly, the eyelids rose, and she looked apologetically at him.

"Oh, Thomas, please forgive me. This illness leaves me feeling so tired at times. I'm not bored, I assure you."

Her voice had never been a strong one, but it now wavered and broke, and she would have to clear her throat. The nurse came in and checked her intravenous drip, took her temperature and blood pressure and nodded to Tom.

"Mrs Laurel, did you still have the bloating feeling after your lunch?"

"Yes, nurse, and the pain down here is a little worse than yesterday. I'm afraid I have had to go a lot today."

The nurse acknowledged the points made and said the doctor would be visiting later. Tom's mother watched the nurse disappear and smiled wistfully, settling herself more.

"Thomas, this must be very difficult for you; your father dying last week and I know I will soon follow him. You will have two funerals soon to arrange. I do so wish you and Kathy would reconcile before I go."

"Mother...*mother*..."

Harold regretted his enquiry as he heard what appeared to be a suppressed sob and clearing of the throat from his companion, and he looked closely at him.

"Um, I must say the Russians really do look after their parks magnificently, don't you think?"

The trite comment allowed Tom to regain his composure, and he nodded and stated: "Quite, though I really cannot say I'm one for spending much time amongst the pansies, what?"

Harold was relieved the conversation was becoming lighter, and he glanced around for another topic to keep the mood.

"Look over there. There's John taking a snap of Novgorod's own Kremlin. You join him, and I'll try and track down Miss Clay and see if she's had any luck finding statues of composers."

Tom watched Harold stride down the path and was surprised to see how sprightly the botanist was moving, especially when he had mentioned his arthritis when bending. Maybe the good weather was drying out his joints, he thought as he approached John. He was happy that the dark mood about his mother was receding, and he tapped his friend on the shoulder, remarking that he was sure there was a bar he had spotted on the edge of the park. John did not need any further encouragement, and they walked for five minutes before seeing an old rundown place with a heavy wooden door. The tables and seats were empty except for a couple of glasses that still had some of the contents in them that confirmed that this place should give them some refreshment.

"I don't know; it is rather rough-looking," said Tom, holding back.

Despite his objections, the two entered the bar through the semi-opened timber door. The interior was dark and appeared empty except for a woman behind the counter. Their eyes took a little time to adjust to the gloom. Rather like the bar in Minsk, a framed portrait of the Soviet Union's recently dead leader looked severely down on them. There were a few chairs and tables although these at least appeared to be made from good wood, rather than plastic.

She greeted them and politely shook her head when they asked for a beer, followed by another when they requested vodka. The woman was amused at the disbelieving looks at what the Englishmen felt were essentials for a Russian bar. She had just poured the last beer and vodka before they had arrived.

"Cognac?" she asked them, finding the relieved expressions on them even funnier.

They watched her go off and the two found a table and waited for her to return with two tumblers and poured them small measures and headed off back to the bar, watching the foreigners drink the cognac. She looked around her and hoped they were not too thirsty. Deliveries of everything were sporadic these days and despite promises from the supplier, she had no beer or even vodka to offer the strangers or her regulars. As a consequence, the bar was getting ever quieter with little for her to do.

She got a signal from the one with the beard who gave her a flashing smile and raised his empty glass. Oh dear, her final bottle of cognac was getting low, but she decided to be generous to these westerners.

She had never had any such visit before, and she much regretted that she could not speak with them and find out more. She believed them to be English or American and tried desperately to recollect what phrases she was once taught at school. Her hands clinched tightly the edge of the counter but nothing came back to her. But then she remembered! A boy in class said that he knew a common explanation in English for when in difficulty. He repeated it several times and she did likewise, committing it to memory. But what did it mean?

As she tried to remember how to pronounce the foreign words, she spotted the bearded man point at his empty glass again. This was an embarrassing moment for her to try and refuse them and say there was no more as well as giving an excuse they would understand.

She approached them and both the men raised their glasses expectantly, the bearded one smiling so beautifully again with those straight white teeth of his and sparkling brown eyes. If only her boyfriend could be like him, and he might have done until he started smiling. It was an affliction that so affected all his family, they were cruelly nicknamed the *Gummy Gorbachovs* by her relatives.

The barmaid stood nervously in front of these strangers who could have been from another world and stared at each of them. The handsome one looked at her with that winning smile and winked, nodding his head, mouthing: "Cognac?", while the other did a strange noise with his lips.

She breathed in deeply and declared: "*Nyet.* Quite honestly, my dick is killing me!"

Chapter Fourteen

The travellers clicked their cameras appreciatively as they entered Leningrad's centre and all were stunned by this European looking city with its classical buildings and canals.

John was immediately impressed, sitting by the window as the coach drove by what seemed to be a shopping district. He spotted a woman in her thirties with long, dark hair and about to enter a shop, staring back at him, and he instinctively smiled and waved to her. She grinned back, waved and then cupped her hand and suggestively used it to hint he should follow her.

"Remember Minsk," warned his friend.

Dina told the travellers more about the history of the imposing city as the coach swept by the great monuments of the centre. In between pointing out the buildings they would visit, including the Hermitage[68] and the St Peter and Paul Fortress[69], her voice grew serious and melancholic.

"I know you will have probably heard of the Siege of Leningrad in the Great Patriotic War, but I ask you to reflect on this. For 900 days from September 1941 until January 1944, the citizens were bombed and starved by the Nazi forces around it. Imagine trying to survive without water, heating or electricity for much of it. We believe 700,000 died, maybe more and so we call it the 'Hero City' for the people's endurance and bravery."

Rick looked at Tom and John, and he mouthed the number of deaths, shaking his head.

"But, dear travellers, we are now in 1984, and I want to show you the beauty of this wonderful city founded by Peter the Great[70]."

The voice that had sounded so full of sadness gradually lightened, and they could see even from a distance, the smile come back to her. The coach passed a large, green building with its Romanesque style as she described how she had thrilled to watch the Kirov Ballet[71] performing Tchaikovsky's *The Nutcracker*[72] there. Dina looked at Rick, expecting a sarcastic comment but was surprised when he nodded back.

"One hell of a nice ballet, lady," he commented, then whispering to the Englishmen, "even though the guy who wrote it was a faggot."

Dina returned to them and Rick shifted uneasily in his seat, wondering if his indiscreet comment had been heard. She looked at John and nodded at him.

"John, I wish to have more words with you, perhaps we can meet early tomorrow evening as I'm free?"

The unexpected request caused John to splutter a hurried agreement, and as she went back to her place at the top of the coach, he tried to ignore his friends' expressions and one comment.

"As the old barbers used to say to their customers: 'Something for the weekend, sir?' Lubrication guar…"

"No, thank you!"

Rick stood impatiently at the hotel reception and looked around him, hoping to see the Englishmen.

He had been happy visiting the great sites of Leningrad, which were more impressive to him than Moscow and gave the feel of a civilised European city. The Hermitage, where they had queue jumped because they had prepaid with hard currency, while the ordinary Russians watched on, had impressed as he wandered the corridors and stood before the Fabergé Eggs[73]. But he had been awed by the visit to Peterhof[74] on the outskirts of the city. When Dina said it had been completely rebuilt after the Nazis had blown it up, showing the images of the destruction, he shook his head slowly, closed his eyes and muttered: "What a people!" He failed to see Dina's beaming smile at his admiring exclamation.

But Rick being Rick, he wanted to see more of life as the Leningraders might enjoy their time at night. He had been disappointed by how little there was in both cities to sit down and watch the world go by, which he found so appealing in places like Paris. With his two companions, he was sure he could seek out some of the unofficial pleasures the place had to offer.

"Hey, friend, can I ask you a favour?" he said leaning against the desk and smiling warmly at the male hotel receptionist. "It's something I need badly while I am here."

The receptionist looked sheepishly around him and then at the American and whispered: "You want a woman for the night? I know some nice, clean ones."

But the American shook his head and raised his eyebrows.

"If you want to change money, I can give you a good rate, sir, but not here."

"We'll come to that, but do you know anywhere I can listen to some local jazz?"

Rick asked the question with a comforting smile but noted the receptionist stood back a little from him and frowned.

"Oh, jazz? You mean *Soviet* jazz?"

"Well, I thought jazz was jazz, but if it has a comrade's rhythm, that's fine by me."

The receptionist coughed and raised a hand, walking away to a colleague and a muffled conversation ensued while Rick tapped his fingers on the counter, spotting the Englishmen and waving them over.

"You guys interested in hearing some jazz played by the Russkies in downtown Leningrad?"

Tom raised his eyebrows as far as they normally could be raised and nodded enthusiastically.

"I am usually one for traditional jazz," he remarked. "It will certainly be more welcome than anything we heard in Moscow."

He looked at John with a smile and stated: "A relaxing evening of jazz in convivial company. What could possibly go wrong with that?"

Sporadic applause broke out in the gloomily lit bar as the musician finished a blues song on an electric organ, stood and bowed to the audience and said in both Russian and English that there would be a 15-minute interval.

While conversation increased among the audience and the cigarette pall grew heavier, a man sat alone and observed those around him, blinking at the smoke that began to irritate him. He held a hand to his mouth and took out a handkerchief, coughing into it. His eyes darted around him, hoping he would not draw any attention to his discomfort. He was there on occasional visits to observe, rather than be the centre of attention and having regained control, he sipped slowly at his glass of beer.

He had to admit that the music didn't greatly appeal to him; he preferred traditional Russian music or if it had to be pop, that which was approved than western rock, which he felt was decadent and discordant. Having said that, when he saw the large framed photographs of the jazz greats – Louis Armstrong, Duke Ellington and in particular, Oscar Peterson, hanging on the wall behind the bar organ, he had to admit a grudging respect for their abilities.

He caught a reflection in the large mirror opposite and looked quickly away. His was not a memorable face, narrow with hair that was beginning to show signs of thinning. The lips tended to be pursed when tense and his long, sallow features were not going to be attractive to many. His intense blue eyes did make people notice, but even here, he tried to stop staring at close quarters.

Instead, he preferred to be an almost invisible witness, and this jazz bar in Leningrad was known to attract western diplomats and business people to relax. It was ideal for him to pick up any gossip or loose talk as the nights wore on, even though he was technically 'off duty'. He was fluent in German, but his English was poor, and in this respect, he had to rely on others to give him a report.

The entrance of a pretty blonde woman clinging on to a chubby, middle-aged Englishman was just what helped him. Natasha – or was she to be Olga for tonight – was perfect for getting useful information and was fluent in a number of western languages. She glanced at him, and he saw the beginning of a smile, which he discouraged by a slight shake of the head that she understood. They would meet a couple of days later for a walk in a park for a catch up. She would hand him tapes or anything else she had gleaned, while he deposited an envelope into her handbag for her reward in helping state security.

He always kept the relationship with the girls at an official level, despite some whispered suggestions to find a little comfort with them. There was too much to lose now with him marrying last year and an important posting to Dresden in the GDR for the next. A fling with one of the girls would leave him open for blackmail by her or one of his colleagues who might get hold of any incriminating evidence.

While he could look forward to his own career going in the right direction, he was growing increasingly concerned at how the country was faring. The death of Yuri Andropov[75] in February, someone who he had particularly admired, had been a heavy blow. After the years of corruption and stagnation, here at last was hope that his leader was launching a purge that was driving out the parasites. But now, he saw a weak and ailing man[76] in place who could barely stand or talk. How could the Americans with all their power take the Soviet Union as a serious competitor now?

He looked slowly around him. It was the usual crowd of jazz loving Russians who could afford the high prices of western beer and spirits and western tourists. As it was the weekend he expected there would be an influx of those he really detested – young Finns on the 'vodka train' from Helsinki who always descended on the city to get blind drunk. Sure enough, five minutes later, the door was thrown open and five Finns staggered in, roaring in English and demanding vodka.

"Hey! Ivan! We want vodka and be quick about it!"

The barman gave them a hostile stare back, but they were already too far gone to care. It was the worst time of the week for him, when he was routinely insulted by the Finns, but his boss told him to keep serving while they could hand over their dollars or Deutschmarks if they wanted to change money in a quiet corner of the bar.

It was seeing this activity near the gents that spurred the observer to finish his beer and look to the exit. He knew changing money on the black market was rife in Poland and some of the other Eastern Bloc countries, but he felt the line should be drawn in the Soviet Union. Yet, he was also aware this bar was useful to gather information and that a crackdown would be counterproductive, so he gave a slight shrug of the shoulders and stood.

He picked up the empty glass and decided to take it to the bar, so he could come close to the Finns and listen a bit more. As he did, the entrance door was opened and three people came in; one was tall with distinctive white hair, another bearded and with a limp and the third, a strange little fellow with an expressionless face and heavyset glasses.

The three were speaking in English, and he could only make out a few words, but as he put the glass on the counter, a heavy hand came down on his shoulder, and he was swung around to see one of the Finns regarding him with bleary eyes.

"Hello, Ivan, I can't let you go. What's your name?"

"Not Ivan," came the response with a weary sigh. "It is Vladimir."

"Where you going, Vlad?"

"Sorry, my English is bad, please, goodbye."

The Finn shook his head and looked around him and spotted Thomas nearby. He snorted and said loudly, suddenly lunging and taking off the Englishman's glasses. "Look, my friends, it's Vlad 1 and Vlad 2!"

Tom looked startled while Vladimir stiffened at the rudeness, grabbing the Finn by his free hand and starting to exert a pressure that led to his adversary gasping, groaning and then sinking to his knees as the Russian continued.

"Okay, Vlad! Okay, Vlad! *Vlad*!"

The Finn handed the Russian Tom's glasses, who in return gave them back to the Englishman who nodded his thanks.

"I…am…I am sorry for this," said Vladimir.

He would have continued but for the first notes on the organ being played by one of the other Finns. It began to dawn on him that this was a jazzy and heavy-handed version of the piece by the composer Sibelius that had been banned by the old Tsarist regime. The Russian heard the dark-haired Englishman mutter: "It's *Finlandia*[77]."

Vladimir glowered at the organist and the other Finns and giving a slight bow to the three tourists, left quickly with his antagonists laughing at his departure and one shouting: "Ivan doesn't like our music!"

Rick surveyed the scene and realised this was not what he had planned for the evening.

"And I don't like the music either, or these jokers," he remarked to the other two. "Hey, who's that I see out there?"

Rick was peering through the window by the entrance door and spotted a familiar figure, making his way quickly on the other side of the road.

"Hey, it's Louis. Maybe he knows somewhere more to our liking. Drink up and let's get out of here."

The young pianist finished his playing of the Tchaikovsky Romance in F Minor and relaxed, giving his usual bashful smile as a smattering of applause greeted the final dying notes on the Becker piano[78].

The piano had arrived spanking new from the local factory, courtesy of an arrangement between the bar manager and his close friend there. A quiet bartering of western spirits from the bar and a night-time delivery of the piano meant both were satisfied by the business done.

Pavel smiled again at the audience and noticed that the older males were particularly appreciative of his performance – as always. He stroked his dark beard and wondered about what next to play while the bar began to fill with more regulars. 'Stroke' was hardly the right word because his beard was so wispy, but the manager had said he wanted him to look like the master composer whose portrait hung behind the piano in pride of place. Pavel glanced at those piercing eyes staring back at him, and he remembered the shocking revelation that an American customer had mentioned to him that Tchaikovsky was a homosexual. At first, he had shook his head and had replied nothing had been said in the

Conservatory and while the relationship might have been a barren one, the composer had at least been married.

But the pianist was curious himself to know about the new disease that was sweeping parts of the USA and which was being described in coverage in the Soviet Union as being common with homosexuals, prostitutes and the homeless.

"We are told this is a western disease," he said. "This thing called AIDS[79]. We can't catch it here."

The American had listened and when Pavel finished, chuckled and put a hand on the Russian's shoulder, giving a gentle squeeze.

"Look about you and ask yourself how many in this bar are from the west?" he queried. "If you can get the clap from unprotected sex now, you're gonna get it from what's to come, if it's not here already."

Pavel was confused about what to think about the subject and himself. He knew what and who interested him, but he also accepted what could be the outcome if the authorities were to find out about him. So much about his life was of trusting but worrying about those he was attracted to and the horror stories of those that had ended up serving hard labour in gulags because of their 'crimes'.

There was also the unreported hate crimes that went around bars like this of violent queer bashing that the police turned a blind eye to. Many were too afraid to even report the attacks because of the nature of what had caused them in the first place. A friend had lent a book published only in the GDR called *The Flying Dutchman* by a Leningrad writer called Vicktor Sosnora. Pavel had read of the brutal death by a gang of thugs of a homosexual academic in a Leningrad bar, watched on and encouraged by a barmaid. The pianist had stopped going into the usual bars for a number of months, but the money he was getting for playing and assurances from the management in this particular place, persuaded him to try and forget the haunting images thrown up by the novel, which even included the murdered man's dismemberment.

Yet he could not forget that here he was in his early twenties on the threshold of potential fame with enthusiastic reports on his progress in the Conservatory. On the other hand, there was the ever-constant worry of what his family would think. His mother was keen to point out the latest girl that had expressed interest in him, while his father more pointedly said after a good few vodkas that he expected to hear he had to get married to avoid a scandal. "I don't care how you do it, just as long as I have a grandson, my boy," explained his father lifting the glass and winking.

As if to offset the memory of the American's words, which were said last year and with all the other worries he had conjured up, Pavel decided to play some Chopin. Unfortunately, the thought of his parents made him lose his way in the Polonaise, but he just about got through the passage with a little improvisation. Reaching the end with some relief, Pavel was pleased his performance received more than the usual applause. He knew as the night progressed he would receive requests to join either a group of admirers or just one, but he tried to tactfully decline by either saying he was going to go back to play or that he was waiting for someone.

It was the second excuse that was proving the true reason. More recently, he was seeing a Dutchman who was making regular visits to Leningrad because he said he was a tour leader of respected groups of academic people. Whether that was true or not was of little concern, but he found the company of this man particularly enjoyable, despite his initial reserve. From time to time, he had looked to the front door of the bar to see if his foreign friend had made an entrance, but although he was expecting, no familiar face could be seen.

The more they had talked about his country, the more Pavel yearned to be able to travel there to see for himself these places. Music was the great means to unlock the door to the outside world and many Soviet artists travelled and performed, even staying in these countries. If he could reach that level, he wanted first of all to play in the Concertgebouw Hall in Amsterdam with its famous orchestra and conductor, Bernard Haitink. And what would he play before the packed hall? He told his Dutch friend he had decided on his favourite concerto – Beethoven's Piano Concerto in C Minor. For the pianist, it was the equivalent of the *Eroica* Symphony, possessing power, reflection and triumph from start to finish.

"My, what a *graceful* performance!"

He looked around and saw an elderly man bowing as he finished the compliment in perfect English.

"I might be able to help you develop your career if ever you're in Scandinavia. Perhaps you can give me your contact details?"

"Are you a director or agent?" asked Pavel, cautiously. There had been many approaches in the past and promises that were never kept.

The man almost pouted his lips and his right hand came up to chest level and the fingers wiggled.

"Let's say that I have been known to make barriers disappear for talented young people like you, even from this side of the Iron Curtain. I understand if you are sceptical, but at least take this card. I assure you I am serious, especially with young and may I say, beautiful artists like you."

Pavel examined the man's card and saw he came from Copenhagen. There might be possibilities, especially when he had described himself on it as an administrator with the royal ballet company there. But when he looked up quickly, there was something in the man's face that warned him to be careful; his smiling was not matched by his eyes that looked calculating.

"Yes, so much to be suspicious about here, isn't there?" the man said, tilting his head. "You can never be too sure in the Soviet Union who is who and what might happen if the guard slips too much. In my city, there are no such, shall we say, constraints. None at all. We are all free to do what and with who we like."

The young man could sense a propositioning was now taking place and he took a backward step, noted by the Dane.

"I see you are not convinced, but I assure you that I have links everywhere in Leningrad and Moscow to make life easier…or more difficult. The first option is always the preferred one for those I have offered to help, especially of *our* persuasion."

This was more than a veiled threat, and Pavel looked around him for an escape from this man whose false smile remained stuck to his smooth, florid face.

"Perhaps we can have more words in my hotel room when you have finished entertaining the audience here?" came the suggestion while the Dane held the pianist's arm. "I'm sure we can find something of mutual benefit there."

Pavel looked around frantically and saw the entrance door open to show Louis, walking in and spotting him instantly. His smile of recognition was warm and so different from the man beside him, and the pianist wrenched the Dane's hand from his arm.

"Oh, I see, the competition has arrived, or is it the Fifth Cavalry?" mused the Dane, sarcastically. "Well, don't worry, dear, I won't create a scene, and I'm in Leningrad for another few days yet. Plenty of time to make an acquaintance," and as Pavel strode away, he muttered to himself, "whether you like it or not."

Pavel found his worry disappear to be replaced by a growing elation as he approached Louis, and they awkwardly shook hands, followed by an embarrassed embrace.

"I'm so delighted to see you here," he said.

"And so are we, buddy!"

Pavel looked beyond his friend and saw a tall, elderly man gazing down at him, accompanied by a little person who reminded him of an actor and director he had seen in an American film recently. Another person with a dark beard stood with him, trying to smile at the scene.

"Oh, Christ!" whispered Louis in Pavel's ear. "They must have followed me."

The Dutchman recovered his self-control and turned to regard the people he last wanted to see in this bar of all bars. Most of all, he tried to stop curling his lip as Rick took in the surroundings and the people with a knowing look and winked at Louis.

"Hey, cute place, my friend. Cute people too. Cute *male* people."

"Mr…Mr…Rick, I didn't realise you find these more cultured places to your taste."

"Come on, Louis, I might seem like a rough diamond, but let me tell you I've been to all the art galleries in Europe," declared the American, folding his arms and grinning to his companions.

"And, no doubt, all in the same day," stated Louis, looking and nodding to Pavel and the others.

"Come on, now, what's with the bitchiness?" queried Rick, feigning to be insulted. "Me and my pals had to gallop to keep up with you. What's the attraction of the place? Where are the broads…I mean, ladies?"

"It's their night off, sweetie," said a man who passed them by, puffing on a cheroot and exhaling ostentatiously from his nostrils. "You'll have to make do with us tonight."

The comment made them all laugh and relax except Tom who found a mounting unease at what he was seeing. The bar was plush by what he had seen so far in the Soviet Union. The mirrors on the wall were ornate and ostentatious, while the tables and chairs matched the kitsch mood. The clientele were undoubtedly more sophisticated in appearance and behaviour. But when he saw the large print of Tchaikovsky and even more, on the opposing wall of Oscar Wilde, something warned him he was going to be in for a night where a seduction by a Russian beauty was unlikely to occur. The print was the famous one of Wilde in a fur coat, sitting, leaning forward with his hand under his chin and looking knowingly at the photographer as if to say: 'Come on, admit it, you're one of our gang too, aren't you?'

The men in this bar were acting in a rather too familiar way with one another, a hand on the knee here and a tickle of the ears there. Nothing he had seen recently in the Civil Service Club near Nelson's Column matched this, but he had hardly been looking for such fraternising there. Rather, it had been the drunken jibes later on in the evening by his colleagues of being 'Tom Thumb'.

Tom moved closer to his friend and gave a diplomatic tug on his sleeve.

"John, I don't want to concern you, but I have a feeling my being compromised is unlikely to happen here on my last night in the Soviet Union. Um, particularly here."

"Unless you want the blond to be without an 'e' at the end…That is, I don't mean *his* end," remarked John, nodding. "But I don't mind if you want to strut your stuff here."

"Sometimes, Murphy, you really…"

"…find me a tasty bit?"

Pavel introduced himself politely to the three westerners and explained, in halting English, that he was the bar's pianist. While he did so Louis scanned the place for seats where they could sit and chat. He had hoped to have some time by himself with his friend but knew that there was little hope now the American and his English companions were there.

These visits with the tour groups were so fleeting and he had to admit unlikely to lead to anything. Yet after two years being coach guide with Astro Tours, this was the first time he had met anyone who showed any real interest in him. The sight of Pavel's smile to him made him forget what was not possible, and he looked again for a place.

"Your turn for the drinks, Tommy," insisted Rick, leading his friend to the bar while the others searched for a place to sit together. "I'll find out what they want. By the way, get something for yourself."

Tom nodded, saying "Thank you" before realising the instruction was not quite as generous as he first thought.

The front door was suddenly flung open and four men barged in. It was apparent immediately that they were not part of the usual crowd. The leader was in his late twenties with short, cropped hair and features that seemed shaped by trying to be like a harsh father and a life with no room for tenderness. Those behind him were pale imitations and held on to one another, swaying as they surveyed the bar. The leader blurted out: *"Time to find our true loves, or let them find us maybe."*

He looked to his left and spotted a diminutive man, who turned and looked at him nervously. The leader approached him and grunted, barking out: *"Come on, darling, give your kisses and arse to me now."* The terrified look by the small man in front of him made him curl his lip, and then he spat in his face, grabbing hold of Tom's jacket lapels.

"I don't like ugly queers like you! Where are the pretty ones?"

The leader's brutal words reached others in the bar, and they fell silent as they recognised what was likely to play out with the gang. He looked at them with a smile that started out almost apologetically but which quickly transformed into a sneer.

"Hello, darlings, guess who's come to make you girls a happy lot? Who wants it? Who really wants it?" He grabbed hold of the elderly Dane who had been attempting to make a discreet exit. A smacking kiss was planted on his cheek, followed by a heavy blow that felled the man.

"Oh, my fucking is too much for you, mate," he stated, snorting and watching his victim on the ground groan. *"Come on, darlings. Who can take it where it really hurts? Let's find out now!"*

The gang spread out to stop any of the customers leaving the bar and watched with great amusement as they shrank back. Only Rick appeared calm as he remained by the bar, leaning an elbow on the counter as he watched the thugs advancing towards the customers.

The leader spotted Louis and Pavel, sitting at a table and came close to the Dutchman. He leaned forward, placed a finger under Louis' chin and stroked it.

"Pretty, pretty boy…but will you look such a stunner after a bit of this?"

From his jacket pocket, the man drew out a knife to gasps and cries of horror from the customers. With his hand carrying the knife, the leader made circles with the weapon, occasionally making darting moves towards the Dutchman's face.

"Now let's see the red stuff!" the thug shouted, only to feel a hand grasping his wrist and a foreign voice whispering in his ear in English.

"Now, I think you've done enough tonight, don't you?"

The Russian broke free and swore at Rick and rushed him only for the American to duck under the weapon and raise two fingers and jab them in his opponent's eyes. An almighty shriek came from the man as he clutched at his damaged eyes and collapsed, kneeling and crying out.

Rick looked around at the nearest thug and grabbed him by the shoulder before giving a karate chop to his neck. His two remaining friends looked at the fallen and unconscious comrade and leader who cried out with his clenched hands to his eyes saying he had been blinded. Any feeling of loyalty deserted them as they went to exit the bar as fast as they could.

One failed to get past the American, and he was picked up like a rag doll before being sent head first into the side of the bar. The sound of the thud was greeted by whoops of joy from the customers as they appreciated their night of horror was being turned into something very different.

Terror had so gripped the last remaining thug that his grasping at the door's handle failed. He looked back and saw the American casually climbing the steps and grab hold of him with both his hands and turn around to the crowd. With a victorious roar, the thug was sent crashing down on to some tables that folded under his weight.

Silence gave way to more applause from the crowd and a bow from Rick until he saw the manager looking aghast at the damage that had been done. Glasses lay shattered on the floor, the contents soaking into the thick blue carpet.

Wondering whether he should take dollars from his wallet, Rick thought again and came to the leader of the gang and went through his pockets, impassively ignoring the moaning. Sure enough, he found plenty of dollars and Deutschmarks there in his bulging wallet and handed them to the perplexed manager.

"Keep the change, sir, and time we skedaddled, my friends," the American suggested, wiping his two fingers with his handkerchief that had so damaged his foe.

The westerners and Pavel hurried outside, looking for and hailing down a taxi. A few quick words were said between the pianist and the Dutchman and the driver was explained which hotel to go to. As the taxi sped away, Louis attempted to express his gratitude. He was still shaking uncontrollably at the thought of what could have happened to him, only to hear back reassuring words: "My friend, don't you remember back in East Berlin I said I would pay you back for me being a pain in the butt? Consider this as keeping to my side of the bargain."

Tom looked balefully in the bathroom mirror and shook his head at what he saw.

The night in the gay bar had left him shaken and even more pale-faced than usual. He cursed he had been persuaded by Rick and John to follow Louis into the place where such violence had occurred. Tom raised his spindly hands in front of him and noted how they trembled still and recollected the queer-bashers had almost mistaken him for one of the local homosexuals. The image of that one thug who had grabbed him by the throat and spat in his face would always be with him, and he shuddered at the memory.

Tom tried to clear his throat and swallowed down the wrong way, leaving him coughing and bent over the basin. He felt a nausea swelling up and wondered if he would either faint or throw up but gripped the sides of the basin as firmly as he could, listening to his friend whistling another Irish rebel song to his disgust.

"Have you finished gargling or whatever you're doing?" came John's perky question from the hotel bedroom. "I've got a date this evening, remember!"

Tom muttered to himself but said aloud: "You just watch it…I tell you, just watch it. Don't expect me to come visiting you in the Gulag after dabbling with Dina."

"Says the honey trap expert," came the sarcastic response.

"Sometimes, Murphy, you really do annoy me!"

John still retained his smile from his friend's predictable words as he closed the door and looked across to where Rick's room was. He had been mightily impressed by the American's martial arts in the bar when he had taken on and beaten the hooligans that had surrounded Louis.

John wanted to find out more, and he saw the door was slightly ajar with some off-key singing heard from the American. He wondered whether to knock but decided to open it and began saying in a heavy Russian accent: "Hands up, capitalist dog! KGB!"

To his surprise, a heavy bath towel was instantly flung in his face and before he could open his eyes, Rick had pushed him back into the dark corridor and shut the door.

"Just knock next time; I'm in the buff, you jerk!" roared the enraged American.

Quickly forgetting Tom's ticking off and Rick's stern rebuke, John walked jauntily into the reception area of the hotel, looking eagerly for Dina but immediately heard a song being given a lilting performance near the hotel entrance.

He saw a mixed group of middle-aged people, the women wearing flowery dresses, while the men had loose fitting grey suits.

"They're Czechs, and they are always singing," he heard behind him.

He turned around and saw a weary-looking Dina gazing at the group that immediately started another song. She had changed from her usual plain dress to a white top and jeans.

A woman from the Czech group noticed their English conversation and came towards them, looking obliquely at Dina and began to sing beautifully to them:

Horo, horo, vysoká jsi,	Horo, horo, you're high,
má panenko, vzdálená jsi,	my doll, you are distant,
vzdálená jsi za horama,	you are far behind the mountains,
vadne láska mezi náma.	love is wrong between us.
Vadne, vadne, až uvadne,	It's faulty, it's wrong when it fades,
není v světě pro mě žádné,	there is no one in the world for me,
není žádné potěšení	there is no pleasure
pro mne více k nalezení.	for me more to find.

When the woman finished, she bowed her head to John and less so to Dina and walked slowly back to the group who applauded her.

"That's superb, do you know what it means?" asked John.

"My Czech is not so good these days, but I have understood the message," came the rather frosty answer from Dina. "Can you wait for me here? I have to do something first."

John nodded and watched her walk towards the hotel entrance. Such was the beauty of the song he had just heard, he turned back to the group, saw the singer beckoning to him and walked up to her. She was younger than the others with a roundish, pleasing face and striking blue eyes, partly covered by long blonde hair that she brushed back.

"I'm so glad you enjoyed the song," she said in perfect English. "Where have you come from?"

"From London. I suppose you haven't had the opportunity to travel to the West?"

"Oh, I have been to London, but it was a long time ago when things were easier."

He noticed that her pretty face clouded over, and she looked down to the floor.

"Was it during what we called the Prague Spring when Dubcek was in power?" he pressed, watching her nod quickly and sigh. "Were you outside the country at the time of the invasion?"

There was another nod and silence before she looked at him and said mockingly with her hand sweeping across her: "But it was thought we had to be saved."

"But you could have stayed in the West," he remarked.

"Yes, but I had things dear to me in my country, and I returned. Those times you speak of have gone."

"They might come back?" suggested John, but he saw a shake of her head, and she started to move away from him, waving a desultory goodbye.

He waved back and thought she probably was aware it was not wise to speak too freely within the hotel. He remembered wryly Tom had given that concerned warning about keeping an eye out for secret police in the bushes outside who might be ready to pounce should he be tempted to let his hands wander with Dina. John well knew from his readings of Solzhenitsyn and other dissident writers, that a suggested walk could be the occasion for conversation to be freer. And, yet he admitted to himself that he hoped on this occasion, maybe, just maybe, there might be something more when he turned and walked towards where he saw Dina.

"We have another Intourist guide who is joining us; this is Boris."

John's lofty expectations came tumbling down at the words, and he looked upwards in expectation of a growling man mountain, only for his gaze to wander down to see where Boris was. Rather timidly, a small, bald man with a large, bushy moustache poked out from behind Dina and grinned, waving his hand that he thrust forward to shake the Englishman's.

"It's very, very good to meet you," said Boris in impeccable English. "My colleague here has said that you are interested in many things about the Soviet Union."

Despite his stature, Boris had a deep, rich voice, and as they made their way to the exit, it was apparent that he had been chosen to ensure there was no likelihood of a romantic tryst during the walk in the forest that evening.

"You have enjoyed your time here in our country, John?" asked Boris, his hands behind his back as he almost marched purposely into the wood with Dina and the Englishman struggling to keep up with him.

"Yes, I have. It's good to see somewhere at first hand and to speak to people directly, don't you think?" replied John, wondering what next question would be raised.

"I am very glad because we feel we are often misrepresented in the West, you know," said Boris, bringing his hands together in front of him and looking earnestly at John. "We deal with many tourists from your country and elsewhere, but Dina says you have asked many questions. More than she has had to deal with on a trip before. May I ask what you do back in England?"

"I'm a journalist."

The crunch of gravel underneath was silenced as both Intourist guides stopped walking abruptly and stared at one another, eyes wide open.

"You're a journalist!"

"Yes, Dina, I am. Does it worry you?"

Dina cleared her throat and nodded her head quickly at her outburst.

"A journalist? You never told me that before. It, um, surprised me, that's all."

"You intend to write about this trip, John? About the conversations you have had?"

"I think you must believe I'm some kind of Fleet Street reporter," the Englishman said with a rueful smile playing on his lips at the thought. "No, Boris, don't worry. I write for the building press, so it's only the way buildings are put together, no more."

"Nothing political?" enquired Boris.

"Only if policies get in the way of the buildings or what's put in them."

"But you like talking about political things, John," observed Dina. "All through the trip I noticed."

"I studied politics and history at university and have kept an interest. I even did a course on Soviet politics and government. Mind you, the lecturer was a person who had never been to the Soviet Union, so his knowledge was a bit, shall we say, skimpy and poor compared to this. Yes, Dr Verity didn't impress us at all. But we had a lady lecturer who had been on an exchange visit to Leningrad and her insights were fascinating...Far more than Dr Verity's. We stopped going to his lectures because he'd just plundered the same books and newspaper articles we'd read already."

"John, I don't mean to be critical of you because you really wish to know and it's a shame this Dr Verity was so poor. But you have only had seven or eight days here. Please, what can you say compared with us who have grown up in our country?"

The Englishman considered Boris's words, and he nodded as the point was made. "But what I've seen isn't quite what the regime here wants to accept exists and that's surprised me."

John proceeded to mention the incidents in Minsk, Moscow and the brawl in Leningrad while the guides listened quietly to his words.

"We may not be perfect, but we have no unemployment…crime…violence," spluttered Boris, his bushy eyebrows dancing with every subject he mentioned.

"…I am sorry to interrupt you, but I've already had this conversation and topics with Dina. As for violence, the bar yesterday wasn't exactly a church meeting."

He watched Boris nod vigorously and then crouch when he saw something near a flower. The guide cupped his hands around a butterfly, brought it up to show his companions with a beaming smile and then let it flutter away.

"You know if you had walked in this forest 45 years ago, you would have been fighting the Nazis," remarked Boris, his face becoming even more serious. "We did not have little skirmishes like your London Blitz but total war. Try to imagine afterwards our world smashed to bits that had to be rebuilt from scratch. We didn't have the luxury of a slowly growing parliamentary democracy like you. And it hurts us when there is President Reagan saying yesterday about bombing Russia. It's as if it's all a joke to him, but look at what it means to us. To call us an evil empire[80] too."

"No, we didn't have an Ivan the Terrible or a Stalin," said John and immediately regretted the remark. "I mean, that our history was different."

"We know Stalin was a man who made mistakes."

"Like the Non-Aggression Pact with Hitler[81]?"

"As much as Chamberlain did at Munich[82]?"

"Touché."

"And I want to say…" began Dina, "…we—"

"We are all victims of those who rule," interrupted Boris, "and yes, with Stalin—"

The three had been talking as they walked down the forest path, which suddenly opened up to a clearing, and just as Boris was about to continue, a policeman came into view and the guide suddenly stopped talking, setting his gaze ahead of them. Dina too fell silent as the policeman walked by without a sideways glance. The incident struck John and he raised both an eyebrow and his hand, gesturing back at the disappearing policeman.

"Why did you stop talking when…?"

He halted as the guides exchanged hurried comments in Russian. While they did he spotted the sight of a familiar tall, white-haired figure gliding among the distant beech trees with another person. Before he could shout, John was distracted by a tug at his shirt and Boris's worried face staring at him with piercing blue eyes.

"I'm so sorry for that, John, but sometimes it's better not to encourage others to know private conversations," explained Boris, his eyes softening. "You know, I think we should turn back or we'll be late back for your last dinner in the Soviet Union. Oh, and that fine free beer Dina tells me you and your friend like so much."

Their conversation became more relaxed on the way back and focused on the sights that John had been impressed with during the trip. Eventually, the hotel entrance came into view and Boris stated he had another appointment with a colleague and bade them good evening. Dina and the Englishman strolled on to the hotel, and it became obvious to him that the Dina who was so animated during the walk was becoming increasingly subdued. This was even more evident when he invited her for a drink at the bar and she barely said a word.

"I hope there was nothing I said that offended you?" he asked after a long silence. "I can be a little too blunt."

"No, no, I am just thinking," she replied, sipping her orange juice and looking quickly around her. "I must go now. Thank you for your time, and I'll see you before you cross into Finland to say goodbye."

Before he could answer, she had quickly raised herself from the chair and left, leaving him even more bemused.

The morning was bright and sun dazzling when Dina entered the coach and looked down to the already boarded travellers who waved back.

She spotted John and gave a brief smile before taking the microphone from Arnaud and wished them all a safe journey.

"I hope you will come back to the Soviet Union one day because there's much more to see."

And those were her final words as she quickly handed the microphone back to the driver without a glance and gave a final wave to the travellers, disappearing down the stairs unaware of the glum look that followed her from John.

"No conquest there, then, what?" said Tom, smugly.

"Yes, something I share with you, Thomas," answered John, a little miffed with his friend's sarcastic observation. "In other words, total failure on the woman front. Your bosses will be almost as disappointed in you as you must be with yourself, *what*?"

Their journey continued until they came to Vyborg, a small town close to the border and where they had the opportunity to change roubles back to hard currency[83]. John decided to hold on to a 1-rouble note for a memento and looked around at the place. It had the appearance of a time warp where the people were dressed in dull, grey clothes and even appeared to move slowly too. The cars and trucks all seemed to be in a style from a 1950s' film; Leningrad was a bustling hive of activity in comparison to this sleepy place.

As he waited in the queue to change money, Dame Edna before him cast a baleful eye around her surroundings.

"I guess you'd see more life in a dried-up billabong than you would here, dearie." she commented. "It's like watching a slow motion picture almost going into reverse."

Dame Edna looked at her purse and tut-tutted, muttering: "What a strange country this is. If it doesn't watch itself, it'll be a riddle turned into a piddle before too long."

John was about to correct her but was brought up quickly by her rising voice, "Oh, I know what Churchill said about Russia, but we speak things as we find them where I come from. Take a good look, little *boorie*[84]. Mark my words, before you know it, this place will come crashing down."

"Remember those wise words," came a voice behind him, and John turned to see Rick nodding his head knowingly as Dame Edna raised her eyebrows and left. "This place is 40 or 50 years behind us. You wait till we get across the border into Finland and see. It's like that episode in *Star Trek* where your man Kirk shags your Brit actress, that broad Joan Collins, leaves her flattened in a street and goes zipping back to the future."

"Oh, no, can't you leave sex behind you for one moment? And were you walking in the forest yesterday with someone?"

"Can I go anywhere you don't know what I'm doing?" asked Rick, coming close to John and squinting. "You burst into my room without a knock. You don't know what I was doing, or who with."

"Your door was ajar, so I guessed even you would show some restraint."

The American thought about what was said and took a step back and looked John up and down.

"You know, you're not bad looking and yet why haven't you got anywhere on this trip? Tom, I understand. He almost runs away when he sees his shadow, but you ain't got the excuses. Maybe it's because you don't have enough of what the ladies want."

"I beg your pardon! I was married."

"Yeah, and your buddy said for just a few weeks."

John made a mental note to give Thomas a good verbal thrashing, but he watched as Rick stroked his chin and make a knowing nod of his head.

"Two problems with you, John. Firstly, you ask all the wrong questions of the girls. Secondly, do what I did, have a steel rod inserted in your man thing."

"A what?"

"A steel rod. It gives enormous satisfaction to the women, John. You just jack it up into the 'ready for action' position and hear the satisfaction for the rest of the night. I'm not saying it's what Romeo did to Juliet, but I tell you, she wouldn't be crying out: 'Romeo, Romeo, wherefore art thou, Romeo?', that's for sure. Think about it, pal," added Rick, patting John on the shoulder and tapping an index finger by his nose. "Stop being intellectual and do anything that gets the women aroused and thinking you got more than the other guy. You're never gonna match that Pip for looks, but next trip, you'll be kicking out poor little Tom from the room and testing those bed springs…to *destruction!*"

The tourists waited patiently by the coach at the frontier post watching the countryside spread out before them and with two massive stretches of barbed wire separating Finland and the Soviet Union going as far as their eyes could see.

The guards had gone at a snail's pace through their passports and luggage before letting them through. One of them had a little grey dog with a constantly wagging tail, and after some encouragement, it started to go through the coach with the guard in attendance. Arnaud watched them sullenly and sucked on his cigarette, looking down and then at John and Tom, tut-tutting.

"You know what they said to me? 'We know you're carrying drugs, Arnaud, and next time we'll get you.' Very friendly, eh?"

"Dina didn't seem very friendly to you either," noted John. "You didn't try anything on, did you?"

"Me? *Me*?" exclaimed the coach driver, raising his arms and looking around him while coming closer to them. "Do you know she hit on me? Yeah! Yeah! When we got past Moscow, she declared she was in love with me. I no joke, my friends. Two trips ago the Intourist guide, well, we slept together. A Latvian, very nice and hot too. Imagine, a very curvy girl comes knocking at your door at midnight. *Imagine*!"

Arnaud paused and a smile came to his face as he recollected the night of passion while Tom smacked his lips.

"But come the morning at breakfast, we were told she was taken ill and had to be replaced," continued the coach driver, a frown getting ever deeper. "They must have bugged the bedroom. They got an ugly bald man called Boris with great big moustache, and I had no wish of bedroom with him, oh no!"

John coughed a little at this but decided to say nothing as Arnaud continued, shaking his head.

"I said to Dina: 'Come on, I drive 10 hours a day and then have to keep Martine happy. It's impossible, even for me, Dina.' She wasn't happy with me, my friends. Not at all. I try to be a good, safe coach driver, but I can't be Superman in bed with two women as well!"

Chapter Fifteen

"Welcome to the most beautiful country in the world!" declared Arnaud into the microphone before handing it to Louis as the coach crossed the border between the Netherlands and Belgium, causing a round of applause from the travellers.

Just as Rick predicted, the trip before into Finland had been like a leap forward in time, as the roads were smooth and the buildings modern and well maintained. Many of the travellers expressed relief, and the sights that followed of Helsinki, Stockholm, Copenhagen and Amsterdam reinforced many of their views, helped along by Rick extolling the virtues of the free economy.

Now in Belgium, Louis delivered his final address over the microphone, stating that he would be coming around with envelopes, which were to show appreciation for the service provided by him and Arnaud on the trip. He emphasised that they were to be marked separately and there was little doubt that most of the tips were going to favour the driver, rather than the guide.

On arrival in Ostend, the coach travellers swirled around both Louis and Arnaud to say their goodbyes, handing their envelopes to the guide and driver with the ones for the latter looking noticeably fatter.

Dame Edna, her friend and the young Australians were particularly gushing in their thanks. Tom watched with barely concealed fury as Pip put his arms around both young girls as they walked and picked up their suitcases with not so much as a backward glance or farewell. He shook his head and grunted as he and John gave their envelopes to Louis and Arnaud. The guide nodded his appreciation, wished them well and walked away to say goodbye to some of the other travellers while the driver nodded towards them in gratitude, saying: "You were good fun. This trip was one to remember. "

"When's the next one?" asked Tom.

"The twenty-sixth starts after I've cleaned out the coach, topped up the beer and wait for the ferry to arrive in a couple of hours," the driver replied, looking a little sadly at Martine who waited patiently for him some yards away. "I don't like saying goodbyes, especially to the girls. They get a bit emotional. Don't know why," he added, sucking on a cigarette and grinning. "But then again, maybe I do. Knowing my luck, Dina will be waiting for me at the Soviet border again. Can't wait for a tour to the Vatican. I should be safe there, boys, I'm too old for the cardinals and Swiss Guards[85]."

As he finished, Harold and Carmen came to him and wished the driver well, handing him their envelopes with Arnaud taking off his glasses and wiping his eyes.

"No tears, friends, just tired from driving you safely to your destination, understand?"

"We may beg to differ because you are a macho man," observed Harold, smiling as the coach driver pushed out his chest and flexed his muscles. "But for a man to drive 10 hours a day and…and…still find time to…to…" His words trailed off as he looked bashfully in the direction of Martine.

"Nothing more than any Greyhound[86] driver could do, pal."

Harold closed his eyes, muttered a few words and turned to face Rick who looked down on him with a wry smile. The American handed over his envelope to Arnaud and looked around him.

"I'm going to miss you guys…All of you."

"One wonders if the feeling is mutual, sir," replied Harold, looking disdainfully at the hand, now placed on his shoulder. "One feels that—"

"Ah, come on, let me buy you all a lunch to make amends," insisted the American, giving the botanist's shoulder a squeeze.

"…One feels that…that…sounds a jolly good idea," stuttered Harold. "I, for one, believe the road to forgiveness has taken a welcome turn!"

"If you want a traditional place to eat great seafood, try *Le Homard Savoureux*. That means Tasty Lobster. See it in the distance over there?" suggested Arnaud, pointing to some old buildings. "Not too pricey but then again, I'm sure Rick will have plenty of Belgian francs to spend on you. And now for the goodbyes, my friends, as I have to clear out the coach."

Firm handshakes and a good deal of hugging occurred until he came to Tom who nervously stretched out his hand.

"Oh, Tom, how very English of you!" declared the coach driver but ignored the hand and still gave Tom a warm hug.

Arnaud walked towards the awaiting Martine and the two came together in the briefest of embraces before he went to collect Louis and the pair approached the coach.

"Holiday romances suck," observed Rick with a shake of the head. "Not that I suppose they were ever a Romeo and Juliet."

"Just a *Brief Encounter*[87]? That can be very romantic but yes, sad," noted Carmen but after seeing the American's puzzled expression, decided not to explain.

"Yeah, when does it really ever work, huh?" asked Rick with a tut-tut.

"Well, I think you are looking at one example where it did," replied Harold with a mischievous smile.

"I know that Pip scored, but I wouldn't call that romance," said Tom with rueful intent. "Just a rutting stag."

"You may look closer, young man," advised Harold, taking Carmen's hand in his own. "But our generation is a little more discreet, don't you know."

Three jaws dropped at once as Rick, Tom and John regarded the elderly couple standing before them, looking lovingly at one another.

"Well, I'll be darned, Harry Potter, you old rogue!" exclaimed Rick, slapping his leg. "It's champagne for lunch, not plonk."

"I have always been called 'Harold Potter', and that's the way I prefer it to remain, dear fellow. But we accept your congratulations, don't we, my sweet?"

"Why, yes, Harold. You mean you had no idea, gentlemen, that a little liaison was forming on our journey?" said Carmen, fluttering her eyelashes. "You really should have spent less time in the bars staring at the bottom of your empty glasses."

The five travellers waited eagerly for the waiter to pop the champagne cork as the elderly couple gazed at one another with a mutual twinkling of their eyes and held hands.

It was a sight that the other three observed with a mixture of amazement. How could they have been so blind to Harold and Carmen's tryst? They had embarked on what seemed to be a physical relationship without giving a clue to the rest of the coach party. Arnaud was expected to be a ladies' man and Pip had all the good looks that were needed to get relatively easy conquests but a threesome must have surprised even him. Yet this aged couple before them, who barely seemed able to put one foot in front of another at the end of gruelling city tours on the route, had managed to fool them all.

A pudgy waiter with waxed moustaches and greased back, thinning hair, looked like a gastronomic Poirot and regarded Harold and Carmen with knowing eyes and nodding head, as he understood romance was blooming at such a late age. He stood before a painting on the wall depicting the room of a Parisian bar where couples were snuggling up to one another with an open bottle of champagne on one table. A man with moustaches similar to the waiter stood alone, while one girl posed before a mirror, and looked into it, thrusting out her breasts and running her fingers through her auburn hair.

Le Homard Savoureux was a good choice by Arnaud with its black, upright piano, a blackboard on the wall opposite with the menu of the day written in flourishes and curly lines; one of the meals depicted a smiling little lamb sticking its head out of a cooking pot. A small fish tank by the piano had oysters and lobsters vying for attention and opposite was a bulging liqueur cabinet made from the finest teak. The tables were all covered in tasteful, patterned linen and at the other end of the restaurant was its heart, a semi-open kitchen where two well-built, mature ladies were busying themselves with the orders. The restaurant was filling with local people, babbling in French and Flemish and a heavy pall of cigarette smoke was already clinging to the discoloured ceiling, adding to the atmosphere.

"I see love is always with us!" exclaimed the waiter, grasping the bottle of champagne and running his hand slowly up and down the neck in what could be regarded as a suggestive way, saying in French: *"Be forever blessed, dear couple."*

While Rick beamed and John smiled meekly, it was Tom who looked even more expressionless at the couple who were, well, a bit like his own parents. Put bluntly, a bit beyond that kind of gallivanting in bed, which people like him should have been doing with the invisible Natasha or Olga on this trip. He squirmed uneasily in the chair, folding and unfolding the serviette, jumping suddenly when the cork bounced off the ceiling and landed in his empty glass to shouts of delight around him, including from other diners.

"Hey, Tommy, maybe this is the bachelor's equivalent of getting the bride's bouquet!" declared Rick, taking the cork out of his glass and slapping the subdued civil servant on the back. The waiter smiled and winked and poured the champagne, which foamed up in his glass and almost dribbled over the rim, only to recede, which Tom found symbolically ironic. He forced a smile that had all the hallmarks of a grimace.

As they were served the substantial fish soup – *bouillabaisse* – for first course, the conversation between them turned to the holiday that was coming to an end. The elderly couple smiled as they talked of their delight at visiting Red Square at night time with that magical sense of seeing St Basil's with those vivid colours.

"Shame the architect didn't get to see much of his work," observed Rick as he squeezed the last bit of flesh from a king prawn and sucked the inside of the shell. "Has to be a tough guy who goes and blinds the creator of such a place. But I suppose Tsar Ivan really was Terrible in many respects."

"Ah, but you must admit Leningrad was a delight," insisted Carmen. "I will always remember the Hermitage and the other glorious buildings."

"You know what I'll remember?" asked Rick, taking a deep gulp of the excellent Chablis the waiter had recommended and then another for good measure.

They waited in fear and expectation that there would be a revelation of some sordid encounter he had arranged with a poor student in his room but watched the American purse his lips and to their astonishment, witness a tear trickle down his cheek.

"It was when we visited Peterhof, and I went into a room and there was a little old lady sitting on a chair. She got up and bowed a little, came up to me and grasped my hand and said in English: 'Peace be with you.' That's what she said, my friends, and you know what? That's when I realised that these Russian folk don't want war. You're lefties, I know, but back where I come from, we get a lot of how the Russians are out to dominate the world. That they're evil. As bad as Korea was, my, that old lady must have been through all the brutality that can be flung at a people. But Lord, 'Peace be with you', now that takes some beating."

Rick finished and took the serviette in his hand and dabbed at his eyes while the group maintained a silence at the unexpected words he had said. Noting the impact he had achieved, a playful smile came to his lips, and he raised his hands and declared: "Now, don't you guys get the wrong idea; I'm still a capitalist and a Republican! Long live Ronnie!"

"Oh, dear, he goes and spoils such a poignant image in Peterhof," replied Harold with a sorrowful expression. "You'll be wanting to sing the praises of Thatcher next."

"You've got a dame with class to whip any arse!"

"My dear Rick, you had entranced us all with your moving experience just a couple of minutes ago," started Harold, wagging his scrawny finger. "But now you have dragged us down to discuss some dreadful woman who would have done us all a great favour had she stayed in her father's grocer shop in Grantham."

"Bit hard on your woman, there, Harold," complained Rick.

"Quite frankly, let me state too about her dance partner, that your President should have stuck with his awful 'B' movies, even after he was out-acted by Bonzo the Chimp[88]!"

"Well, it's true that he was no Humphrey Bogart," conceded the American. "I'm talking about Bonzo now…I'd be mad to rate Ronnie as Oscar star quality."

The quip caused the group to relax and enjoy the rest of the meal as they tucked into creamy fish fillets followed by rich desserts with Rick generously ordering more wine and lacquers as the sweets arrived. Tom looked increasingly mellow as he regarded the double whisky, constantly pushing his spectacles back into position and occasionally doing his trademark lip smacking. The frequency and noise of the action were beginning to concern John as he was aware that more of his friend's meal was finding its way not into his mouth but on to the table mat.

"Might I raise a glass…I note a rather empty one, to our host?" stated Tom, looking closely at the lack of whisky. "I feel that it is the least he…I mean, we can do to celebrate the end of this journey."

"Don't you think…?" began John, nervously.

"…Indeed I do, often, *hah*! But I will say to *mein* host that while we are poles apart in most respects, we have shown we can strike up a rapport…especially when the glasses become fuller," observed Tom, squinting at his glass.

"Tom, that's a bit rude; Rick hasn't bottomless pockets," said John.

"When it comes to my pal, Tommy, his cup runneth over," contradicted Rick, leaning across the table and patting Tom on the shoulder. "Remember when you said in Berlin that you didn't consider me a pal?"

"I…that is…I may have been premature in my assessment," said Tom as the waiter came and poured a good measure of whisky into his glass. "Which I realise now was completely…that is to say…premature."

"And who was there for you when you were caught with your pants down?"

"I do believe it was you," agreed Tom, staring ahead and reliving the moment before drinking deeply. "My dignity was rather compromised on that occasion. And you were my rescuer in the gents' toilet in Moscow."

The others looked at each other bemused by Tom's statement but catching their mood, Tom added with a firm voice: "I wish to make clear there was no cottaging or, indeed, any act of gross indecency occurring in said gents...After all, I'm British, not gay!"

"But Tommy, what about that Oscar Wide fellah?" queried Rick. "Now there was an English gent for the stable boys."

"He was Irish, a Dubliner," corrected John. "He just spoke like an English toff. But he was married with two children, so busy at some time with the female form."

"And a well-known masturbator while confined to Reading Gaol," confided Tom, slurring. "It is a practice that...that...I, for one..." and Tom fell silent as he failed to wonder what next confession to highlight.

While Rick nodded at the unexpected information, it was fortunate that Harold was whispering in his true love's ear and smiled as she quickly nodded at his words.

"You know, Tommy, I doubt if you'll even remember me if I passed you in the street or was sitting by you on the bus in a couple of months' time," Rick declared, hoping to move off the subject of what used to occur in Reading Gaol.

"I will tell you, sir, that would be impossible!" exclaimed Tom, pointing his finger in the way he usually reserved for John. "My memory will always hold your image there. Even if you were dressed as my favourite film star, Sophia Loren, I would spot you for who you really are."

Rick looked around him and muttered: "Marilyn Monroe?" He was grateful that Harold was about to announce something.

"My friends, if I might call you that, we would like to invite you all to our wedding at Chelsea Registry Office. The time is not set until we get back, but I trust it will not be too long. We are treating this as our honeymoon, but I am certain we will find a place where we can reciprocate Rick's wonderful generosity. And now..."

They applauded the elderly couple as Harold took Carmen by her hand and led her to the piano. The waiter, who had been hovering, had heard the news and beamed as he opened the lid and brought a chair for her to sit down.

"My voice may not be quite in its prime for hitting the high notes," declared Harold. "But we do believe we have just the song for this happy occasion!"

The waiter clapped his hands and the restaurant fell silent as he stated: *"Ladies and gentlemen, listen, please. This beautiful couple will soon be getting married in England, and they want to sing a song for you!"*

The customers burst into applause and waited for the botanist to clear his throat while Carmen played a dexterous introduction to a song from *My Fair Lady*.

I'm gettin' married in the morning,
Ding, dong, the bells are gonna chime
Pull out the stopper, we'll have a whopper
But get me to the church on time…

Soon the restaurant was echoing to clapping in time and to a surprisingly strong voice singing in a Cockney accent all the way to the end with a faultless accompaniment on the piano from Carmen. The song ended to a thunderous ovation from the customers and cries of *"Encore!"* ringing out and causing the ladies to halt working in the kitchen and peek out.

Harold bowed while Carmen did a modest curtsy but could not be persuaded to continue, while Rick stood and applauded, walking towards the piano and smiling at the customers.

"What music! And what can follow that?"

The waiter translated but with an increasingly worried expression on his face as it occurred to him he knew precisely what the brash American had in mind.

"Well, yes, *mes amis*, I know and I ask you what can be better than what you've just heard. But how about this across the Atlantic from the greatest nation in the world just for you l'il ol' Belgians?" asked Rick, sitting down at the piano and waiting for the waiter to finish the translation, only to hear:

"Non!" (No!)

"Geen!" (No!)

"Now you don't mean that, folks, cos you owe us G.I. guys one for the war," said Rick, beginning to play some notes forcibly, "and this is why!"

Yes, there were times, I'm sure you knew
When I bit off more than I could chew,
but through it all, when there was doubt
I ate it up and spit it out
I faced it all and I stood tall

And did it my way!

"Oh, Jesus wept! Wouldn't you guess he would pick that one?" asked a muttering Harold as the cooks stopped peeking, the customers watched stony-faced while the American completed the song and stood, looking around him till his eyes rested on the glum botanist.

"See, Harry, old bean, sometimes a stunned silence shows more appreciation than applause!"

Epilogue

Tom sat bolt upright in the chair outside Worsthorne's office and looked at the smug face of the incumbent Home Secretary still propped against the facing wall, noting he had a worst comb over than he did, which gave him little hope for the coming years.

He had been back two weeks from the trip to the Soviet Union and been expecting a call to recount how he had evaded the Russian blondes and any other lures on the hostile side of the Iron Curtain – or had not. On his side, the hope had been he could tell them how he had rebuffed the attentions of a Marta in Moscow and a Larisa in Leningrad in a way that Sean Connery had so badly failed as 007. But what if he had to tell them he had succumbed? That Margarita in Minsk had wrapped her silky legs around his wiry torso while he fumbled to open the dusty packet of prophylactics by his beside? Or that a Nina in Novgorod had urged him to attempt a Volga boatman position to please her *yet again*?

But the reality was that the nearest he had come to being compromised was by Julia in that tacky club in West Berlin and Wanda the transvestite in Warsaw. Of the Soviet Union and its entrapments, there had been none.

He shook his head sorrowfully as he contemplated having to tell his bosses the abject truth that his being seduced by the enemy would have to await his next visit. Just the thought of seeing all those countless onion domes again almost brought tears to his eyes as he determined to go anywhere else in the world. In fact, he had told John on their return that the whole of the Eastern Bloc was his alone to visit for the foreseeable future.

Most of the night on his return from the trip had been spent going over the holiday, and he concluded there was little he cared to remember. The other part of the nocturnal hours was getting used to the sounds next door, although to his surprise he heard: *"Oh, God, Damian...! Oh, God, Damian...!"* Followed by: *"Urrhh, Tasmin! Urrhh, Tasmin!"* There must have been a change of occupancy while he had been away to account for the different names, but the ecstasy and noise levels remained irritatingly the same.

As he continued mulling, he failed to notice someone had arrived and was sitting near to him. It was only when he was called into Worsthorne's office by his boss, Morrison, that as he stood, Tom caught sight of an elderly, bald man with tufts of white hair here and there on his pate, pale long face and dull, grey eyes. The man nodded at him as he did back and turned to follow his superior into the office.

The door was shut and Worsthorne sat behind his desk, examining a newspaper. His superior finished reading the article before glancing up and motioning Tom to sit. He continued looking at another item in the paper and frowned before giving a big sigh.

"This bloody strike is dragging on forever!" he exclaimed to Morrison. "They'll never win but if NACODS[89] goes ahead after the ballot to strike, the brown stuff will really hit the fan, and it won't be lignite[90], what?"

Worsthorne looked around him to see if his clever joke had resonated but seeing two bemused faces, looked down again at the newspaper.

"Leon is most perturbed that if the pit deputies walk out, we might have to sue for peace. Just imagine Scargill's face if that happens. No secret this, but there's talk of sending in the army to guarantee coal movements. All sorts of contingencies being laid on Margaret's table but if we don't watch out we might actually see the trades union movement coming right behind the NUM. This whole bloody dispute could split the country right down the middle."

"See the opinion polls only give the government a 5% lead as well," said Morrison, tapping the side of his face with a biro. "Neil Kinnock PM isn't beyond the bounds…"

"…It's more serious than that, Charlie," interrupted Worsthorne, placing his hands under in his chin and falling momentarily into silence. "Do you realise that they might get the ministries working *together* if the crisis develops?"

"Good lord!"

"Yes, there are rumours that we might be brought together in some emergency committee with the MoD, DoE and even Social Security to cut the benefits to striking miners' families…and…"

Worsthorne stopped abruptly. It dawned on him that he had said too much in front of Tom, and he squinted at him, his face beginning to go red and almost plethoric, hissing: "Thomas, dear fellow, you haven't heard a word of this, have you, because if anything comes back, I know where you work…Or put another way, where you once would have worked."

"No, sir, I, that is, I can only remember you motioning me to sit down," replied Tom, relieved to see the colour fade and a smile appear on his superior's face, followed by a nod towards Morrison.

"I see one ray of sunshine, Charles."

"And what's that, Frank?"

"Look at the front page here," declared Worsthorne, picking up the paper and showing the front page main photograph with a huge smile. "Charles and Diana have named their second lad 'Harry'. Well, Henry Charles Albert David, to be precise. Christening in December. Hope he shows a bit more brains than the first one. Seems a bit dim to me when he's put before the cameras."

"Erm, frankly, this latest one doesn't look very much like the father," observed Morrison, peering closely.

"No, that's what I thought. Ginger hair, doesn't look a Windsor at all. Now, now, we're like the bloody gutter press!"

"Glad to see my first name's got a mention though. If only my last name had been Stewart, Frank."

"Charles Stewart? Now, that royal had a rather sudden end, so stick to keeping your head in the Civil Service," advised Worsthorne who suddenly fixed his eye on Tom. "Well, one hopes you don't mind all this banter, Tom, but we didn't drag you in to hear a load of tosh between us so…How did your trip go to good old Bolshie Land, eh?"

From being totally peripheral to the discussions that had allowed him to look around at the heavy brown furniture and wallpaper, along with the smell of cigars and whisky, Tom found himself suddenly brought back by the question.

"Um, very well, thank you, sir."

"Live up to expectations?"

"Well, we saw an awful lot during the time."

"Didn't bump into that treacherous bugger, Philby, while in Moscow, did you?" enquired Worsthorne, savagely. "We gather he likes going to some bloody Georgian restaurant."

Tom considered what his response should be, and he was aware that he was in danger of those tell-tale beads of sweat appearing and blurting out too much for no point.

"Let's cut to the chase, shall we? Were there any attempts made to compromise you by any of their ladies?"

It was Morrison who had asked the blunt question, and he saw a pained expression on his subordinate's face, followed by a desultory shake of the head and mumbled words: "Afraid not."

"Well, by any males, then?" enquired Worsthorne.

"No," answered Tom, suppressing the thought of the incident in Leningrad and his comment in Ostend. "I really am not of that persuasion, sir. I'm British, after all."

"Well, you obviously didn't go to the same public school I went to. So, all our worries were unnecessary?" mused a disappointed Worsthorne to Morrison. "You see, Tom, what with your previous work in Northern Ireland and your current responsibilities monitoring the IRA and their fellow travellers here, we thought you might be subject to some interest in your business. As you know, our red friends have been very sympathetic to the republican cause over in Ireland."

"By the way, how is your work going on the republican groups here?" asked Morison. "Didn't get around to reading your latest report."

"I think we have seen the likelihood of any bombings like in Birmingham or Guildford behind us, sir," declared Tom, clearing his throat. "I believe the security forces have done a good job infiltrating the cells and breaking up the ones that are operating here."

"I see, so Maggie will be triumphant on the subject in her conference in Brighton next month," noted Worsthorne with a smug look spreading over his face. "Keeps her off our back on that subject anyway. Only got the miners to see off now, what?"

"One doesn't want to tempt fate – and I'm not a betting man normally – but I think she'll be able to sleep well in Brighton while she's there," predicted Tom confidently.

"Good man. You see, Charles, with that quality of intelligence we can say young Thomas will find himself taking a few rungs up the ladder in the Home Office."

Morrison nodded and moving towards the door, showed that the meeting had reached a satisfactory conclusion, giving Tom the thumbs up sign and opening it for him to walk by.

"Make it Bangkok next year, and we won't need to bother you, eh?" suggested Morrison, winking and then nodding towards the man who had been sitting near Tom outside the room.

The way the meeting had gone left Tom ecstatic and those final jocular words from his boss was a suitable seal of approval as he inadvertently bumped into the elderly man who smiled back gently.

"Very sorry, I must be careful where I'm going," remarked Tom, continuing jauntily down the corridor.

"Well, if only he had shown that on our trip," said the person with a gentle American accent and watching the disappearing figure affectionately.

The man grinned at Morrison and continued into the room where he was greeted with an outstretched hand from Worsthorne and offered a seat.

"Presume you'll have a Bourbon, Teddy?"

"I was beginning to get used to vodka but maybe it's time to fall back into my old ways," joked Teddy.

The American looked around at the room and waited patiently for Worsthorne to add ice and then a generous slug of Bourbon to the glass and bring it to him. Morrison came and sat by his boss, and it was clear that the English civil servants were eager for a spilling of the beans.

"I'm glad my disguise was a good one for your colleague as I must say the journey was, shall we say, revelatory for me, especially playing 'Rick'. You know there were three things that helped – getting involved in drama at Princeton University as a student, damned good make up with fake tan and wig," continued Teddy, patting the top of his head. "And those false soles and heels added to my stature as well as providing some useful storage space," he stated, pointing to his shoes. "I almost got caught out when Tom's friend walked into my room unannounced in Leningrad and I scooted to the bathroom. And I'm afraid the thespian in me got me sailing close to the wind with the other travellers. Couldn't help but playing to the gallery and there were a few who really did hate me for being the yakerty Yank."

"But besides living the part, you got what Henry wanted?"

"I did, Frank, and maybe a bit more. It's a very interesting place and the people I met gave me the information I needed to pass on."

Teddy watched as he observed Worsthorne moving about on his chair like some child getting too excited and wanting to hear more of the story. He found English civil servants he had met a strange mixture of good minds affected by what he thought was an education that constricted rather than encouraged the character. But it was in a way an entertaining experience with them and one that he would miss.

"Now, Teddy, I must say that the luck of finding you through Henry was a stroke of immense genius on my part," confessed Worsthorne, modestly. "After all, MI6 was longing to make contact with their agents in the USSR directly and you could keep an eye on our young Thomas. Two birds with one stone."

"And we know Tom was in need of a little protection," stated Morrison. "He gets a bit squiffy and talkative after a few and vulnerable. Or that's what we thought."

"Well, as you know being on secondment to MI6 is my last assignment now that I'm retiring" – and the American looked at his watch – "I do believe from 23.59 hours tonight. It's the first time I've had an assignment and a holiday combined, except last year prior to the Grenada business[91]."

"You were naughty boys for not telling Maggie about that little escapade," declared Worsthorne, wagging his finger at Teddy.

"Yes, not Ronnie's finest hour, but he seems to have her cooing now, so all must be forgiven," the American acknowledged, sipping on the Bourbon and rolling the glass in his hand.

"So, after today, I suppose you'll be heading back to the States and putting your feet up?" asked Morrison. "No family to worry about either. Lucky blighter!"

"Oh, the world's my oyster, and I've always believed in travelling light. I'm going to flick this coin and decide," added Teddy, taking a 10 pence piece and tossing it, noting where it landed in the palm of his hand. "Yup, that's where I'll head…to my Shangri-La. Gentlemen, if what I've said about Thomas coming back intact in mind to our satisfaction but alas, still untouched in terms of his body, has satisfied you? Well, then, I'll be on my way."

Worsthorne and Morrison nodded and beamed back, standing as one and the senior official came from behind his desk and approached the American, beaming and shaking his hand.

"It's been a pleasure dealing with such a consummate professional, Teddy. I'm sure your last mission has been a great success and one we will *never* forget."

As John closed the door behind him, he noticed the thin, light-blue-coloured airmail letter on the floor and bent down to retrieve it.

He had just returned from another of those boozy business functions at one of the posh hotels that the industry PRs were so fond of holding to impress both their clients and the trade hacks. As usual, the food fell short of anything memorable while the drink was always flowing.

The product launch of the 'unique' and 'revolutionary' range was unveiled, led by the marketing manager's breathless explanation as to why it would lead the market and the company's competitors. "As the boiler system is to be targeted at areas where coal has once been dominant, this offers customers secure supply in the current climate," he started obliquely. "You could say it's a win-win situation, even though Mr Scargill won't be a happy man."

It was also a cleaner system as it used LPG (Liquefied Petroleum Gas), he added, showing his 'green' credentials to great effect during the slideshow demonstration. "We are entering an era where everyone should realise that we ignore the future of our planet at our peril. Our company is determined to play its role in this mission – or as our CEO, Maurice D'eath, has so aptly coined – 'Let's Glorify Greenness'. I can guarantee to this audience that our emissions are well under control," he concluded.

"Unlike his fucking own," whispered a fellow hack next to John.

There were a few cursory asides on his trip to the Soviet Union by his peers, and he duly explained why he felt the country was not quite the ogre portrayed. As the liqueurs were placed on the table, he began to accept he was pampered and spoilt compared with what he had experienced a month before.

"Must have been a bit grim there, John," observed Nigella, the PR's assistant, lifting the Port glass to her mouth. "I gather the people aren't friendly and isn't it the country with all those queues? Give me Rimini anytime!"

John considered explaining why he believed the comparison was a false one but a look at the woman convinced him to remain silent. With her heavily made-up face, loud voice and darting eyes, it was clear to him that her observation was not for contesting. She had already started a conversation with another journalist from a bigger title without waiting for his answer. John opted on accepting the free wine and let the inevitable haze descend.

"Let's face it, Murphy, if you had to choose between the capitalist system and the communist one, which one would it be, eh? Why are you bloody here anyway? Sure *Pravda*'s got a vacancy for a red like you from the west."

The caustic jibes came from one of the more senior journalists who delighted in pointing out John's apparent contradictions while stroking his moustache.

"Why should I have to leave my own country in its time of need, Denis?" came his subdued reply.

"What 'time of need'? The economy's booming and look at property prices. My place has gone up 30% in value over the last year."

"Trouble is, so have those around you and this is going to be a bubble that'll burst," stated John, beginning to rise to the challenge. "You just wait and see what will happen to Lawson[92] and his boom when the economy goes tits up."

He had employed the same words in an Irish pub he used, when the jobbing builders who were making a small fortune out of the yuppies on their house moves, challenged him on his views.

"You're living in the past, Murphy," chastised Denis, peering into a generous glass of cognac. "You watch, this is going to be a golden age. Especially once Maggie's sunk the miners."

John had downed as much as he thought wise for the journey home. The PR man saw his rueful gaze and came up to him, making it clear he approved of the decision to go on the Russian trip.

"You know, I'd love to see the other side, John. *Vivre la différence* and all that. Sure, you're right; they're not thirsting for war. But it's Hazel, you see, she'd not be so keen and how would we keep the kids interested? When they've flown the nest, perhaps. Or if I'm really lucky, Hazel's found another nest before then!"

As he stepped out of the hotel, John noted that a few doors down, a rough sleeper was setting up his place for the night in a shop doorway and another two were already wrapped up further along. The man looked at him and gave a toothless grin while John looked back uncomfortably.

The braying from Denis was ringing hollow, even in this place in London. He passed by a street vendor waving a copy of *The Evening Standard* with its headline: 'Maggie Bashes Brussels'. John conceded few people were willing to listen to Jeremiahs like him.

Now, back at the flat, he wondered who the letter was from and looked at the back for the sender's name. It was from Vera, and as he opened it, he thought back to that visit to the hard currency store and how naïve was her delight to have the western-made bra.

He read through the letter but found the writing was difficult as it was spindly and compact.

'Hello John. It is me, Vera, the girl you met in Moscow. You were kind and took me for a very nice lunch. You took me to that shop and we got that recording machine. It has been very good and helped me a lot in studies. And then you didn't mind I got bra too. Thank you. Did the rest of your trip go well? I like Leningrad. It has many big buildings and is prettier than Moscow, I think. You got back to London safely, I hope? Now I study a lot with little free time and I want to study more English so I can write better to you. When you have time, please write to me and maybe say when my English needs to be better. I will not mind. Maybe you will come to Moscow again and we can spend more time for me to show you more than hard currency shops. I promise! Please write soon. Your friend, Vera.'

John re-read the letter as he made himself a cup of coffee and pondered what he should do. He had thought about revisiting the Soviet Union, flying this time but with the idea of going to the republics in the Caucasus. Thomas had made it clear he would not be a part of another trip there, even though John insisted there were bound to be exotic beauties that would be ready to pounce in Azerbaijan, Georgia or Armenia.

He put a tape on of a recently bought performance of a Shostakovich symphony he was fond of and came back to the letter on the table by the window. John looked out on the familiar road with children returning from school and admitted to himself that this was the place he knew best. This was a country where the likes of a Toby and Jasmine would rule the roost selfishly for many a year. But what alternative would there be for him now his career was heading somewhere?

He was sure that Vera was miles apart in character from Ewelina, but there seemed little possible hope there would be a chance with all the distance between them. And there would be mountains to climb with Soviet bureaucracy to get Vera over here, even if a relationship developed between them.

John left the letter on the table and searched in the fridge, fumbling for a can of beer as the final hushed notes of the first movement of the symphony sounded. He nodded to himself, grunted, tore up the letter and threw it in the bin.

Harold supped deeply at the gin and tonic, smiled and looked around at his pristinely kept garden with great contentment.

He placed the glass on the little table by him and persuaded himself that one more measure from the bottle would do no harm. Yes, late September was proving to be an Indian summer in more ways than one.

Back from the Soviet Union, Carmen made no delay in moving in with him in his Hampstead home, bringing her upright piano. She was now playing some of her favourite Schubert songs transcribed by Liszt. The melodic notes reached him and his smile became greater as to how life had taken a miraculous turn for the better.

He had been a lonely widower for 10 years and had thought any chance of a romance was well behind him but then along had come Carmen. Who would have thought a packaged coach tour could throw up such a charming match? Now he had more to look forward to than tending his beautifully kept garden with its impressive apple tree.

His thoughts returned to the trip. It had almost been ruined when he allowed himself to become outraged by Rick. Yet even he, despite his obvious shortcomings as an American, had proved to be more substantial than the botanist had thought.

True to their word, Harold and Carmen had sent out wedding invitations for November to Rick, John and Thomas. While the young men had replied that they were delighted to accept, he had yet to receive a response from Rick. Harold thought it strange that the American had written down a forwarding address but decided it was up to him if he made a show or not.

"Letter for Mr Potter!"

He looked to his right and saw a smiling Carmen approaching, waving the letter and he took it, kissing her hand gently. Was he being an old fool or was she looking even younger these days, living in sin with him? Those thin hands with pronounced blue veins appeared plumper and softer to his lips. What did it matter, as they were happy together, he decided.

"I do hope my music isn't disturbing you, Harold?" she asked, concerned.

"If music be the food of love, play on!" he replied. "Please, it's delightful, my dear."

She nodded and walked back to the drawing room and soon he heard those glorious sounds of one great composer's reworking of another's compositions. As if in answer to the moving performance by Carmen, he heard a nightingale trilling, and in the background, bees could be detected, humming between his deep red geraniums. Maybe he could persuade Carmen to play a little of his favourite English composers, Elgar and Vaughan Williams, after their high tea with scones, Devonshire cream and homemade raspberry jam.

Harold looked down at the typewritten letter and opened it. Resting it on his lap, he contemplated the generous contents in the glass he had poured for himself. His smile broadened as he found it hard to believe that this sunny, autumnal day could have ended so perfectly, or even be bettered. Yet it was just about to be.

Picking up the letter, he read its contents with mounting anticipation. It informed him that his third love – after Carmen and botany – was to be rewarded. He had become accepted and welcomed as a full member of the Joseph Stalin Society.

Teddy looked for a No 24 bus that would take him to near Hampstead Heath and smiled as he thought about Worsthorne's last words to him.

He had prided himself on being the consummate professional throughout his career in the CIA, no matter what the job was or how unenthusiastic he had been when ordered on to a mission that left him uneasy. His time in Latin America, which included dealing with the *Escuadron de la Muerte*[93] in Salvador, had made him question the morality of what he was doing. But then he found himself arguing that as a patriot, it wasn't for him to question.

This last mission to make contact with dissident agents in Minsk, Moscow and Leningrad, under the guise of a tourist on a coach trip, had been a breeze in comparison. Protecting his strange companion, Tom, was an entertainment that he was likely to remember with a smile on his face for many a year. That he had sat a couple of hours ago next to him without the Englishman knowing who he was, could have been down to a testament of the American's disguise and acting skills or Tom's myopia.

The story he told to the English lads on the coach was fake. He had never been married. There had been a good number of relationships with women from around the world but leading nowhere when he suddenly had to disappear at the end of a mission very much as he had arrived. The one in Chile was particularly poignant, and it was a sad day when he had to let Pinochet's *Dina*[94] secret police know his mistress's whereabouts to lead them to some other regime opponents. She, like them, were all carted off to the notorious Chacabuco camp to be tortured. Teddy winced at that memory as he took out a scrap of paper with a few instructions, realising he was coming to the bus stop where he had to leave.

Children were dancing by him, and he had to tell a couple to watch out for him as they ran down the pavement. He saw them hurtle along without a care and a sense of envy and a wish that they could have looked to him as a father swept across him. But this was not the time to be sentimental, and he approached the empty telephone box and looked at his watch before entering it and smiling when the phone started ringing, picking it up and hearing: "So good to see you home again."

He replied in faultless Russian: *"This is to let you know the bald eagle has landed, and he has news of the eaglets ready for when he flies to his new nest."*

Teddy put the receiver down and quickly took out the one-way airplane ticket to Moscow he had received in the morning post-dated for the following day. As he was doing so, he remembered another communication and took that out, squinting at it. Of course, he had forgotten about Harold and Carmen's big day and regretted he would be unavailable. But as he had handed back the wig and shoes to MI6 with false heels and soles, his lack of hair and stature might have posed too many awkward questions. He replaced the invitation in his jacket pocket before opening the phone box door.

The American looked both ways and saw the next group of children scurrying down the pavement and smiled as they passed by him without a care in the world. One girl dropped a little toy bear near him, but as he reached to pick it up, heard the young voice shout: "Leave it alone, you ugly old man, or I'll call the police!"

His eyes widened and jaw dropped in dismay. He prayed there would be no similar rude advice in the language he had been learning intensely for the previous six months and hoped to use after his flight landed the following day at Moscow's Sheremetyevo Airport.

THE END

End notes

Forward

1. **The Eastern Bloc** – was the international group of communist states that was directed by the Soviet Union during the Cold War between 1947–1991 against capitalist countries dominated by the USA.

2. **Marxist-Leninist** – a hybrid socio-economic belief drawing on the writings and statements of German Karl Marx and Russian Bolshevik leader, Vladimir Lenin. The goal was reaching a communist, classless social system, i.e. common ownership of the means of production and distribution with full social and economic equality of all members of society. The suppression of alternative points of view tended to come from when Lenin grabbed power in the Bolshevik led revolution in October 1917.

3. **Berlin Wall** – Probably the most visible example of the Cold War, the Berlin Wall – for the most part, two walls – was constructed by the regime of the German Democratic Republic (GDR) to stem the flood of its citizens getting to the capitalist Federal Republic of Germany (FDR). Begun in 1961, it had watchtowers and obstacles in no-man's land, a potential death trap for those trying to escape between the two walls dividing East and West Berlin.

4. **Margaret Thatcher** – Without doubt the dominant politician in British politics during the 1980s and Prime minister from 1979–1990. Her right wing political views, including an anti-trade union policy – 'the enemy within' – and virulent anti-communism, saw her dubbed as the 'Iron Maiden' by one minor Soviet journalist, Yuri Gavrilov, as early as 1976; it was a nickname that she embraced warmly. Her monetarist policies

led to soaring unemployment and many would argue that the Falklands War against Argentina in April 1982 was her defining moment as well as saving her from electoral defeat. Thatcherism, where mass privatisation of industries and services occurred, along with the vote winner of the right to buy of council homes, saw the high-water mark of her reputation. Abroad, she was lauded by right wing regimes and behind the Iron Curtain, Thatcher was regarded as having almost saint-like properties. Poland in the early 1980s was a case in point. Solidarity looked to her as she did to them as the first possibility of bringing down communism in Europe. By 1984, when Thomas and John travelled to the Soviet Union, her position appeared invulnerable until her own parliamentary party brought her down in 1990 over the huge unpopularity of the poll tax, along with her increasingly authoritarian leadership.

5. **Ronald Reagan** – President of the USA from 1980–90, like Thatcher, an ultra-conservative with a great dislike for socialist leaning attitudes at home and abroad. Making his name as a limited Hollywood actor, he became Governor of California in 1966 and eventually a successful Republican presidential candidate against Jimmy Carter in 1980. He launched a programme against the unions at home and instigated an arms race against the Soviet Union abroad, enlisting an enthusiastic Thatcher along the way. His description of the Soviet Union as 'the empire of evil', which would be 'consigned to the dustbin of history', was treated as rhetorical hogwash by many but proved accurate. The Soviet Union was crumbling with an ageing leadership and collapsed, bringing down the whole communist bloc.

6. **Intourist** – The official state travel agency of the Soviet Union, Intourist was founded in 1929. It was responsible for managing the great majority of western foreigners' access to, and travel within, the Soviet Union. Its holiday tours tended to be less expensive than western travel companies with its own guides on the coaches throughout the trips.

7. **Iron Curtain** – after his surprise defeat in the UK General Election in 1945, Winston Churchill delivered his historic speech in 1946, in the USA, when he declared: "From Stettin in the Baltic to Trieste in the Adriatic, an iron curtain has descended across the continent." This observation was before Soviet leader Joseph Stalin installed communist

regimes in most of the countries the Soviet armed forces had driven Nazi Germany from during the Second World War.

Chapter One

8. **KGB** – The intelligence security agency for the Soviet Union until its collapse in 1991. It was responsible for both espionage and other activities abroad and internal security domestically. The KGB had substantial powers that allowed it to operate as a state within a state.

9. **David Bailey** – A celebrity photographer since the 1960s, David Bailey became internationally famous for his work and for being David Bailey, with a string of affairs, including with the fashion model, Jean Shrimpton (credited with wearing the first miniskirt) and he married French actress, Catherine Deneuve.

Chapter Three

10. **Woody Allen/*Annie Hall*** – The controversial American director and producer had made his name as a serious cinematic figure with the film *Annie Hall* in 1977, which saw him and his then lover, Diane Keaton, win a number of Oscars. Unfortunately for Tom, his appearance was strikingly similar to Woody Allen, so much that he would often have people calling out the name of the American whenever he walked into a pub or down a street.

11. **Concorde** – The British-French turbojet-powered supersonic passenger airliner made an impressive debut in 1969 but with seating for only 92–128 passengers, it was judged an expensive plaything for celebrities and businessmen. The plane was withdrawn from service in 2003. It was not the first civil supersonic plane, having been beaten months before by the Soviet Union's Tupolev Tu-144, sarcastically nicknamed 'Concordski' because of its resemblance to Concorde.

12. ***Giovanni's Room*** – James Baldwin's 1956 novel deals with the traumas that confronts a white American coming to terms with his sexuality when he falls for a male Italian bartender in Paris. Baldwin's own

problems were immense for besides being homosexual, he was a black activist and intellectual in conflict with the racist attitudes in his native USA.

13. **Ian MacGregor** – Scottish born, MacGregor will always be remembered for his role of helping break the miners' strike of 1984–85 as chairman of the National Coal Board. He had built up a reputation as a hard, anti-union boss in the US and was merciless in his cutting costs at British Steel in the UK prior to taking on the miners. His appointment was seen as Thatcher's first step to dealing not just with the NUM but trade unions more generally. In both, his role proved pivotal. He received a knighthood for his achievement in 1986. When MacGregor died of a heart attack in 1998, his passing was greeted with little regret in the mining communities. NUM vice president and fellow Scot, Mick McGahey stated: "It's no loss to people of my ilk. MacGregor was a vicious anti-trades unionist, anti-working class person…I will not suffer any grief, not will I in any way cry over the loss of Ian MacGregor."

Chapter Four

14. **Trabants** – If there could be a bigger contrast between West and East Germany, it was seeing the modest Trabant versus the sleek Mercedes on the autobahns. Citizens of the GDR had a 12-year waiting list to get their hands on the two-stroke little vehicle. Their leaders decided cars were a low priority for the centrally planned economy. This was in contrast to the Soviet Union, which had a decent export market for the Lada to the West, along with Czechoslovakia and its Skoda (which translated means 'Too bad' or 'Pity', which could have applied more accurately to the humble Trabant).

15. **Fred Flintstone** – From the popular cartoon television series that was launched in 1966, the bumbling Stone Age man still had all 'mod cons' in his life.

16. **Sergeant Bilko** – a popular wheeler-dealer character in a 1950s' US television show. Bilko had no scruples, tried to have a finger in every pie but was often betrayed by his own ineptness.

17. **Solidarity** – Founded as the first independent trade union in the communist bloc in August 1980, Solidarity gained massive support in the population tired of mounting scarcity of goods and authoritarian rule, reaching 10 million members in its first year. It was suppressed on 13 December 1981 when martial law was declared. However, the decade ended with it recognised by the regime, and it was instrumental in destroying communist rule in Poland.

18. **Warsaw Pact** – Founded in 1955 as a response to western powers establishing the North Atlantic Treaty Organisation (NATO) in 1949, the Warsaw Pact was the military equivalent of the Soviet Union and communist countries in Central and Eastern Europe.

19. **Pope John Paul II** – Karol Józef Wojtyła became Pope John Paul II in 1978 and played a huge role in helping the opposition to communist rule in Poland. Rather strangely, the communist regime invited Pope John Paul II to the country and it set in motion forces it could not control. A controversial figure for his mainly conservative teachings, he died in 2005 and was made a saint in 2014.

20. **Czechoslovakia 1968** – The so-called Prague Spring, which was led by the progressive government of Alexander Dubček, caused huge alarm in the Soviet leadership. With other Warsaw Pact countries, Czechoslovakia was invaded on 20–21 August 1968. Dubček's hope of 'socialism with a human face' was brutally smashed and the country was not to see any significant progress until the end of communism in Europe in 1989.

21. **Lech Wałęsa** – An unemployed electrician in Gdansk, Wałęsa had been involved in many disputes prior to the founding of Solidarity in August 1980. His force of personality saw him quickly become the main leader in the movement that soon was seen as challenging the communist regime. In December 1981, he and thousands were rounded up when martial law was declared. During his 11 months of incarceration, he was awarded the Nobel Peace Prize and despite being portrayed as a rabble-rouser, all attempts by the regime to discredit him failed. In the end, he was released, and with the fall of communism, he eventually became President of Poland in December 1990. More of a rebel than statesman, Wałęsa was judged a failure in his time in office.

22. **NORAID** – Formally known as the Irish Northern Aid Committee, NORAID was seen as a front for funding republican paramilitaries – principally the Provisional IRA – during the Troubles in Northern Ireland from 1969 onwards.

23. **Erich Honecker** – A hardline communist, Honecker assisted in achieving the highest living standards in the Eastern Bloc. But he continued a mass surveillance of the population with the aid of the dreaded secret police, the Stasi. In the end, the regime was totally dependent on the support of the Soviet Union. He regarded the changes that the Soviet leader, Mikhail Gorbachev, pressed for with great suspicion and regret. When the GDR collapsed in 1989, Honecker avoided prosecution in a German court and ended his days in Chile, dying of liver cancer in 1994.

Chapter Seven

24. **Wojciech Jaruzelski** – While Poland struggled with mounting debt and lengthening queues, Jaruzelski rose to take power in 1981. He had been the General who suppressed illegal strikes in 1970, and in December 1981, he declared martial law. It was thought at the time that without taking this step, the Soviet Union and allies would have invaded as they had done with Czechoslovakia. In the end, he came to accommodation with the Solidarity leadership, which paved the way to the first free elections in 1989. Jaruzelski escaped punishment and died in 2014 following a stroke and other medical problems.

25. **Douglas MacArthur** – One of the most controversial figures of his time, the five-star General and Field Marshal of the Philippine Army against the Japanese, was lauded during the war. MacArthur's role was queried after the war in Japan when he appeared to go beyond his remit, but his downfall came against then President Truman during the Korean War, which started in 1950. MacArthur was hugely popular with the American public, but Truman still believed MacArthur was deliberately flouting his authority and had to go. Both men suffered from the tussle, but the military man's reputation was held dear by many, especially by veterans of the Korean conflict like Rick.

26. **Pemex shops** – Similar to the Beriozka shops in the Soviet Union, these hard currency stores were first opened in 1972 and allowed Poles with the means to get hold of goods that were difficult, if not possible to obtain in Poland. By the early 1980s, these and a massive black market for hard currencies, especially the US dollar, made the country's economy even more distorted. Pemex shops disappeared after the collapse of communism.

Chapter Eight

27. **Kinks/*Lola*** – A popular British group of the 1960s and 1970s, the Kinks had a great hit song, *Lola*. It described the meeting of a young man with a transvestite in a Soho bar and Ray Davies, main singer and songwriter of the Kinks, was coy whether it was an encounter by him. Rick's rendition would have been appreciated by the coach travellers, if not Tom.

28. *Casablanca* – The 1942 romantic Hollywood film with the unforgettable quotes and performances from Humphrey Bogart, Ingrid Bergman and others. This quote by Dina alludes to a drunken Rick – played by Bogart, not this novel's character – bitterly remembering how Ilsa walked out on him in Paris.

29. **Byelorussia** – Now called Belarus, the then Soviet landlocked republic was devastated by the Second World War, losing an estimated 25% of its population. Its capital, Minsk, had over 80% of its buildings destroyed in the conflict.

30. **Leonid Brezhnev** – Leader and General Secretary of the Communist Party of the Soviet Union from 1964 until his death in 1982, Brezhnev was the most dominant figure since Stalin. Replacing the erratic Nikita Khrushchev, he will be remembered for a period of economic stability domestically in the 1970s but which deteriorated through a lack of investment. A series of poor harvests saw the country becoming more reliant on foreign grain imports. His suppression of the dissident movement was also pursued rigorously throughout his time in power. Corruption and a stagnant economy were to blight his later years in power. Internationally, he reached a series of missile agreements with

the USA under Richard Nixon in the 1970s and the term *Détente* described the superpowers' relationship. However, he was condemned for the invasion in 1968 of Czechoslovakia and the disastrous intervention in Afghanistan in December 1979. Brezhnev's failing health was evident for a number of years before his death in 1982 of a heart attack.

31. **Young Pioneers** – The Soviet equivalent to the Boy Scouts and Girl Guides, the Young Pioneers was seen as a vehicle to help assist with the image of Soviet youth as a positive force in the emerging socialist system.

32. **Great Patriotic War** – From 1941–45, the Soviet Union was locked in a brutal and titanic struggle against Nazi Germany and its allies. About 80%–90% of Axis forces were tied down on the Eastern Front and Stalin evoked heroes from the past in Russian history, along with tolerating the Orthodox Church, to join in the war against Hitler. Approximately 30 million are estimated to have died in the conflict.

Chapter Nine

33. **Wes Hall** – The fearsome West Indian fast bowler struck terror in many an English cricketer during his test career that lasted from 1958 to 1969.

34. **Beefy Botham** – Ian Botham gained legendary status for England when he singlehandedly turned around the fortunes in the third test match at Headingley in 1981 against Australia when all seemed lost. England went on to win the test series.

35. **Lincoln Steffens** – The American journalist came out with his famous statement: "I have seen the future and it works" after a visit to the emerging Soviet Union in 1919. It is often forgotten that his enthusiasm waned as Stalin tightened his dictatorial grip on the Soviet Union.

36. **Hungarian Uprising** – The imposition of hardline policies in Hungary, which had seen cuts in living standards as well as suppression of civil liberties, eventually led to demonstrations initially by students in October 1956. After a period of violence, there appeared to be an agreement domestically to resolve differences. What the Hungarians had not taken into account was a sudden change in attitude by the Soviet

Union leaders, led by Nikita Khrushchev, that saw the return of the Red Army and crushing of opposition. Behind the *volte face* was the fear that Poland – where a demonstration had been put down earlier that year – and other states in the newly created Warsaw Pact would declare neutrality and fatally wound Soviet control in the region. The military action led to thousands of communists in the West resigning from their parties. In the UK, the Communist Party of Great Britain saw thousands like Harold Potter leave in disgust at what they believed was naked repression.

37. **W.B. Yeats** – While Yeats is revered for his poetry, his politics are another matter, especially in the 1930s when he allied himself with the Blueshirts, an Irish fascist movement. An unashamed elitist, he hated the left leaning mass movements. His short poem, *The Great Day*, exemplified his views. Was Harold Potter being ironical in his quote to John?

38. **SPD-Liberal Alliance** – Formed in 1981, the Social Democratic Party (SDP) – led by former, disaffected Labour Party luminaries of Roy Jenkins, David Owen, Shirley Williams and William Rogers – and the Liberal Party, believed an alliance would offer a serious challenge to the then unpopular Thatcher government and weakened Labour Party. It came close in the 1983 General Election as Tom points out but went into a decline as bickering between the SDP leadership and the Liberal Party started to lose its appeal with the electorate. An eventual merger between the Liberals and SDP into the current Liberal Democratic Party occurred eventually in 1989. (The first attempt in 1988 had the tail-wagging-the-dog name of the Social Democratic and Liberal Party (SDLP).

39. **Beamer** – A dangerous ball in cricket, which is bowled without bouncing and is above waist height.

Chapter Ten

40. **Gulag** – The system of prison camps established in the new Soviet Union. It became active while Lenin was alive and soon filled with those seen as not friendly to Bolshevik rule. The gulags were increased

massively under Stalin with estimates suggesting that over a million died in them during his time.

41. **Stalin** – Referred to earlier in notes, Joseph Stalin was a Georgian who came to power after the death of Lenin in 1924. Aware that Lenin warned about Stalin's ways, the assumption of power took time and involved the removal of adversaries like Trotsky. By 1929 as General Secretary, Stalin was in effective power and the 1930s saw the cult of personality develop along with mass purges. The invasion by Hitler in 1941 could have seen Stalin toppled, but in the end, it was the Nazi leader who was defeated. Great swathes of territory gained by the Red Army there and along with the USA clearly the other main gainer from the conflict, the world was set for the Cold War. Stalin's reign ended in 1953 with a cerebral haemorrhage coincidentally on the same day as the Soviet composer, Prokofiev died, ironically of the same cause. After a power struggle, Nikita Khrushchev emerged victorious and set about dismantling many of the harsher aspects of life in the Soviet Union.

42. **GUM Store** – The famous store – which faces the Kremlin on Red Square – had approximately 1,200 shops before the 1917 revolution. It was nationalised and its fortunes plummeted under Stalin when it became office floor space. It reopened as a department store in 1953 and proved popular with visitors with queues often going well into Red Square.

43. **Andrei Tarkovsky** – The famous film director who fell out of favour with the regime, produced atmospheric works like *Solaris* but eventually left the Soviet Union and lived in France until his death in 1986. Conspiracy theorists believed his lung cancer was caused by the KGB and that his wife and sound designer suffered the same kind of disease while shooting the film *Stalker* in 1979.

44. **Aleksandr Solzhenitsyn** – Solzhenitsyn was the leading Russian writer of his time with a number of works that exposed the cruelty of the Soviet system under Stalin. Refused publication in the Soviet Union, his literature was published in *samizdat* form (clandestinely). His masterpieces included *The First Circle*, *Cancer Ward* and *One Day in the Life of Ivan Denisovich*, which was published with the approval of Nikita Khrushchev in 1962. A victim himself of the gulag, Solzhenitsyn was deported by Brezhnev in 1974 and continued writing. His works

became more polemical and his own views increasingly eccentric, focusing on criticising the western ways for its decadence and the failures, as he believed, of post-Soviet Russia.

45. **Novodevichy Convent** – The Novodevichy Convent is in the south-western part of Moscow and was founded in the sixteenth century, housing many ladies from the Russian nobility who were coerced to 'take the veil'. It was shut as a convent by the Bolsheviks until the war with Nazi Germany and was allowed to continue as a religious institution after 1945.

46. **Beriozka shops** – Ordinary Soviet citizens were not allowed to have foreign currency, which is why the store assistant shouted out to Vera that "Russians are not allowed here". The so-called hard currencies – US dollar, West German Deutschmark and the Pound Sterling – were accepted and later, western credit cards. These shops were only to be found in the major cities where western tourists and business people were present, offering goods that were almost impossible for the likes of Vera and her parents. They died out once communism collapsed and the rouble became a convertible currency.

Chapter Eleven

47. **Yuri Gagarin** – Gagarin became the first man to go into space and orbit the earth on 12 April 1961. It caused shock in the USA that it had been beaten by its Cold War adversary and admiration around the world. Gagarin was feted wherever he went, and when he came to Britain, he was greeted enthusiastically, including in the open top Rolls Royce, which Harold Potter saw. A giant in what he achieved, the Soviet cosmonaut was only 5 foot 2 inches tall. He died in a plane crash in March 1968.

48. **US moon landing** – In 1969, the USA landed two astronauts on the surface of the moon. Rick's point scoring was that the Soviet Union could not match the spending and commitment to get a manned mission originally boasted by President Kennedy in September 1962.

49. **Zil limousine** – Produced just outside of Moscow, the Zil limousine was almost entirely for the Soviet élite. The last was manufactured in 2012 when all production of vehicles was stopped.

50. **Zil lanes** – Introduced by Brezhnev in the 1960s and disliked by the ordinary Muscovite, the so-called Zil lanes were for high-ranking Party officials and other functionaries in the centre of the major highways of the capital.

51. *Animal Farm* – Published in August 1945, George Orwell's allegorical *Animal Farm* tells of the corruption of a revolution by farm animals against their farmer but ends up with the pigs imposing a brutal control. In the end, the rest of the animals can't tell the difference between the pigs and the farmers they have invited to a party. Not surprisingly, the novella was banned in the Soviet Union.

52. *Kolkhozes* – After the 1917 Revolution, the regime pushed for the establishment of *kolkhozes*; collective bodies of farm workers. Under Stalin, this became a forced measure, leading to resistance from many peasant farmers.

53. **Winston Smith** – The anti-hero character in Orwell's *1984* novel who vainly tried have a personal battle against the system personified by Big Brother. That and many other allusions to Stalin's Soviet Union, led to the novel being banned in 1950 and was only allowed to be published after 'editing' in 1990.

54. **Ministry of Truth** – The department where Winston Smith worked where truth is, in fact, turned into lies if it suits the state.

55. **Room 101** – The place of torture. All citizens' fears are known to the state and as Winston finds out when he is broken in that room, it's his terror of rats.

56. *Plov* – The Uzbek equivalent of the rice-based dish pilav.

57. **Henry Cooper** – The popular British heavyweight boxer who twice fought Muhammad Ali unsuccessfully in 1963 and 1966. Cooper was particularly known for cutting easily, which happened in both bouts. Less celebrated was that he often was in a horizontal position on the canvas, i.e. knocked out, which is why Tom felt a kinship with the boxer.

58. **Khinkali** – A large Georgian beef and pork dumpling, often served on a platter and shared.

59. **Sonny** – The full codename for the infamous Kim Philby was 'Sonny, Stanley'. A British Intelligence Officer. Philby was part of the 'Cambridge Five' who supplied the Soviet Union with highly sensitive documents and information during and after the Second World War. He was recruited by the Soviet Union in 1934 but worked as journalist up until 1940 when he joined MI6, the British counter intelligence department. Although suspected as a double agent, the cover was only blown in 1963, but he defected to the Soviet Union before being apprehended. Philby was roundly condemned as a traitor, and he lived in Moscow in relative obscurity until his death in 1988. His fourth and final wife was a Muscovite and weaned him off alcohol and dealt with his depression. The *Aragvi* was said to be his favourite restaurant.

60. **Beatles, *Back in the USSR*** – Released in 1968 by the Beatles, it was banned by Soviet authorities, along with so many western pop songs but listened to avidly by many of the young generation there. The regime's description of the Beatles said it all – 'the belch of western culture'. However, in an allowed tour of the Soviet Union in 1979, Elton John insisted on performing *Back in the USSR*, despite officials requesting he didn't.

61. **Lubyanka** – Originally built in 1898 as the headquarters of the Rossiya Insurance Company, this neo-baroque building was where victims of purges and any other cooked up charges were brought by the secret police (then called the *Cheka* and later the KGB). It now houses the successor to the KGB, the Federal Security Service (FSB).

62. **Chaika** – The Chaika limousines were rather like a Bentley to a Rolls Royce, one step down from the Zil, which was exclusively for highflying Party officials but still for the very privileged, e.g. regional governors and their associates.

63. **Fidel Castro** – The charismatic leader of the Cuban Revolution, held power from 1959 to 2011. He was seen as a huge challenge to US dominance of the region and President Eisenhower imposed an

economic embargo in 1960, which is largely still in place. The Cuban missile crisis in 1962 almost caused a nuclear war when the Soviet Union attempted to install missiles on the island. Castro retired in 2008 and died in 2016. There were many, verified attempts on Castro's life by the US secret intelligence agency, the CIA. As the Cuban leader loved to smoke his Havanas, one of the most bizarre is said to have included an exploding cigar that would have been delivered on one of his visits to the UN in New York.

64. **Soviet rock concerts** – The regime frowned on rock music as decadent but by the early 1980s realised they might control some elements. The KGB even used to organise 'official' concerts but still came down hard on clandestine, unapproved ones that were played in out of the way places.

65. **Mensheviks** – Sasha is showing how he and his friends played a clever game by keeping the authorities 'sweet' on an official line but subversive on another. The word 'Menshevik' in Russian means minority, but this term was used by the 'Bolsheviks' (majority) when there was a split in London during a meeting of the Russian Social Democratic Labour Party in 1903. The February Revolution in 1917, which overthrew the Tsar, proved a missed opportunity in ending the war with Germany for the Mensheviks and their allies, which Lenin and the Bolsheviks exploited and led to the October Revolution. Lenin suppressed the Mensheviks in 1921.

66. **Mushroom gathering** – A favourite pursuit of Russian and eastern European peoples, Tom may either have been thinking of this or perhaps alluding to 'magic' mushrooms as he fell under the spell of the "funny-funny" cannabis cake.

Chapter Thirteen

67. **Sergei Rachmaninov** – Born into a wealthy, aristocratic family in the Novgorod region, Rachmaninov was a late romantic composer and pianist who left Russia forever after the 1917 revolution. He settled in the USA and died there in 1943. Like his compatriot, Glazunov, his music was regarded as out of step with the trend to more dissonant music

of the twentieth century, especially compared with the compositions of fellow Russians Stravinsky, Shostakovich and Prokofiev.

Chapter Fourteen

68. **State Hermitage** – Originally founded in 1754 by Catherine the Great and including the former residence of the Tsars, the Winter Palace, the Hermitage is the second largest museum in the world after the Louvre and is one of many attractions of the city.

69. **St Peter and Paul Fortress** – Peter the Great founded the fortress in 1703 to head off a feared attack by Swedish forces. In its way, it became as a big a symbol in pre-revolutionary thought as the Bastille did in France for alleged repression by the Tsarist regime. The site was severely damaged in the siege of Leningrad by the Nazis and had to be restored. Now a museum, it is a great tourist attraction, including its impressive Peter and Paul Cathedral.

70. **Peter the Great** – Regarded as probably the greatest Russian monarch, Peter the Great founded St Petersburg in 1703 as part of his reforms to modernise the country and to his own importance.

71. **Kirov Ballet** – Originally founded in the mid-eighteenth century, the Mariinsky Ballet was changed following the assassination in 1934 of the Leningrad communist leader, Sergey Kirov, with some thinking Stalin had ordered the killing of a potential competitor. The ballet company reverted to being called the Mariinsky Ballet after the fall of communism and end of the Soviet Union in December 1991.

72. *The Nutcracker* – First performed by the Mariinsky Ballet in Saint Petersburg in 1892, *The Nutcracker* had mixed reviews, not because of the music by Tchaikovsky but the choreography and a number of the dancers. It has, of course, gone on to be one the world's favourite ballets.

73. **Fabergé Eggs** – Despite his French name, Peter Karl Fabergé was born in Saint Petersburg in 1846 to a German father and Danish mother. Inheriting his father's jewellery business, Fabergé gained fame through the creation of his jewelled eggs, the first being made for Tsar Alexander III in 1885. A total of 69 eggs were made until the Revolution in 1917 with 52 surviving.

74. **Peterhof** – This incredible palace was Peter the Great's answer to Versailles. Completely destroyed by the Nazis, it was meticulously rebuilt and remains one of the highlights of the city and its surroundings.

75. **Yuri Andropov** – While determined to drive out corruption in the Soviet Union when he assumed power following the death of Brezhnev in 1982, Andropov was no liberaliser, either socially or economically. He had been ambassador to Hungary at the time of the uprising in 1956 and head of the KGB from 1967 and a leading caller for the invasion of Czechoslovakia. As head of the KGB, Andropov was ruthless in his persecution of dissidents. Nevertheless, after the mendacious Brezhnev years, he was seen as a strong man willing to tackle corruption. His health was fragile, and he died in February 1984.

76. **Weak and ailing man** – Andropov's successor as General Secretary of the CPSU was Konstantin Chernenko. Seen by Vladimir in the jazz bar and by many others in the country as not up to the job, Chernenko was effectively a dead man walking with multiple health issues. He died in March 1985.

77. *Finlandia* – The tone poem by the Finnish composer, Sibelius, was performed in Helsinki and could not be performed by its original title to avoid offending the Russian regime because it was thought to be subversive. Finland's relationship with Russia and the Soviet Union was often a fraught and violent one.

78. **Becker piano** – Becker was a well-known piano manufacturer based in Saint Petersburg, which continued production after the Revolution but not to international standards.

79. **HIV/AIDS** – The first case of HIV/AIDS in the Soviet Union was in 1984, but this was removed from the records. The authorities persisted in claims that this was a 'western disease' and no real moves were made to drawing up a plan to deal with this until after the collapse of the Soviet Union.

80. **Evil empire** – Ronald Reagan made this famous speech to the National Association of Evangelicals in March 1983, describing the Soviet Union as an "evil empire". Before the UK House of Commons in June 1982, Reagan also talked about consigning communism to '"the ash heap of history". Boris and others in the Soviet Union believed sincerely that the real aggressive intentions rested largely with the leaders in the West.

81. **Non-Aggression Pact** – The Pact, which was signed in Moscow on 23 August 1939, came as a total shock to the outside world. How could the leading fascist country make a deal with an ideological foe? For Stalin, the fact that the western powers had turned its back on Czechoslovakia at Munich the previous year was good enough reason. However, secret clauses to the Pact meant the Soviet Union would be able to walk in without challenge from Nazi Germany to the Baltic republics, including Finland as well as carving a part of Poland for itself following Hitler's invasion of 1 September 1939.

82. **Munich Agreement** – Hitler's success in occupying the Rhineland in 1936, an illegal occupation of Austria later in 1938, led to what he said was the 'final' demand of incorporating the Sudeten Germans within the borders of Czechoslovakia into the German Reich. No matter what can be said in defence, it was seen as a collapse of will by Britain, led by Neville Chamberlain and France with Daladier and a betrayal of the Czech people. On 23 September 1939, the Munich Agreement was signed between France, Britain and Germany as the main players and paved the way for Czechoslovakia's dismemberment. The fateful words, on his return to Britain, by Chamberlain of "peace in our time", was to pursue him to his grave in November 1940.

83. **Hard currency** – As communist countries like the Soviet Union did not allow its currencies to be traded on the open market, a strange economy developed where hard currency, e.g. US dollars and West German Marks, allowed luxury and quality goods to be bought in beriozka shops. Demand from Soviet citizens encouraged black market operators, despite the threat of criminal prosecution. Western tourists were often pestered to change their money, and as they were supposed to declare how much hard currency money they had coming into the country and buying roubles, they were supposed to exchange them back at the official rate.

84. *Boorie* – An aboriginal term of endearment for 'baby boy'.

Chapter Fifteen

85. **Swiss Guards** – The Pontifical Swiss Guards were established by Pope Julius II in 1506. With their distinctive dress uniform, all have to be

unmarried Swiss males between the ages of nineteen and thirty. Arnaud's cynical reference to them and cardinals comes from the rumours and scandals that circulated about the widespread homosexual behaviour in the Vatican.

86. **Greyhound** – The famous North American intercity company's origins began in 1914 but adopted its name in 1929. By 1983, Greyhound had a fleet of 3,800 buses, dominating the US intercity bus travel market with 60% of all customers. There are numerous songs recognising it, including Chuck Berry, Simon and Garfunkel and John Denver. No wonder Rick sung its praises.

87. *Brief Encounter* – The 1945 British romantic film directed by David Lean involves an unconsummated relationship between two married people played by Trevor Howard and Celia Johnson. However, while they clung on to their respectable status, Harold and Carmen were proud not to.

88. **Reagan's 'B' actor** – Always lampooned for his acting ability, or lack of it, Reagan never made the grade and had to settle for a string of 'B' movies, culminating in notoriety with *Bedtime for Bonzo*, a tale of a chimp being taught moral values by a psychology professor. Many thought Bonzo outacted Reagan in the film.

Chapter Sixteen – Epilogue

89. **NACODS** – the National Association of Colliery Overmen, Deputies and Shotfirers (NACODS) was primarily involved with the safe operation of the coal mines. Without its agreement, no mine could carry on operations. It was crucial during the 1984–85 miners' strike and was bitterly dismissed as one of the reasons it failed because it would not back the fight against the NCB. One sarcastic comment was that NACODS really stood for the 'National Association of Can-carriers, Obedient Dopes and Suckers'.

90. **Lignite** – Often known as 'brown coal', lignite is soft and brown, combustible rock formed from naturally compressed peat. Worsthorne was referring to its properties and human waste.

91. **Grenada invasion** – The invasion of the Commonwealth independent country occurred on 23 October 1983. A hastily led combined US and

Caribbean force was determined to intervene when the leader of the Grenadan government, Maurice Bishop, was ousted in a coup and executed. Reagan said he would not tolerate 'a bunch of leftist thugs' taking over the island. Although a Commonwealth country, Reagan did not inform his chief ally, Thatcher, until the invasion was underway. The USA was condemned in the UN for what was regarded as an unlawful act but appeared to have support from the Grenadan people.

92. **Nigel Lawson** – Chancellor of the Exchequer at the time of the boom time in the UK economy between June 1983 to October 1989, Lawson was seen as instrumental to the Thatcher revolution of deregulation, particularly the so-called 'Big Bang' in the London Stock Exchange and privatisation of nationalised industries. The speculative rise in housing and inflation saw a loss of control of the economy that led to another recession. Lawson had resigned just before the bubble burst.

93. *Escuadron de la Muerte* – Literally meaning Squadron of Death, the gangs ran riot in El Salvador and were funded and supported by the right wing government and rich landowners. No one who was a critic of the regime was safe, including Archbishop Oscar Romero who was assassinated as he gave mass in 1980. Weapons were supplied by the USA, even though it was known how brutal the gangs were. Similar death squads operated in other Latin American countries.

94. *Dina* – Officially known as the *Dirección de Inteligencia Nacional*, *Dina* was more accurately called Pinchet's Gestapo. Established after Pinochet's coup against the democratically elected President Allende in 1973, the secret police set about imprisoning and torturing all those perceived to be the regime's critics.